# When WEREWOLVES Attack

# When WEREWOLVES Attack

## A Field Guide to Dispatching Ravenous Flesh-Ripping Beasts

DEL HOWISON

**Ulysses Press**

Published by:
Ulysses Press
P.O. Box 3440
Berkeley, CA 94703
www.ulyssespress.com

ISBN: 978-1-56975-733-8
Library of Congress Control Number: 2009943781

Printed in the United States by Bang Printing

10 9 8 7 6 5 4 3 2 1

Acquisitions Editor: Keith Riegert
Managing Editor: Claire Chun
Editor: Richard Harris
Editorial consultant: Clay Martin
Proofreader: Lauren Harrison
Production: Judith Metzener
Cover design: what!design @ whatweb.com
Cover illustration: wolf © istockphoto.com
Interior illustrations: Miro Salazar

Distributed by Publishers Group West

*To my wife, Sue,*
*who puts up with my daily transformations*
*and*
*To the boys—Mike Uggla and Dave Willoughby:*
*Long may you run.*

# Contents

The best dream is living a life wherein everybody assumes you are something other than you really are.

# Introducing the Lycanthrope

You are driving down a country lane in the silvery light of the full moon when suddenly you round a curve and come upon a horrific sight. Something big, black and covered with fur hunkers in the roadway, its snout buried in an oozing heap of . . . what? Looks like a load of laundry that has been slimed by an oil spill. The beast rips away a chunk and stands up. It's even bigger than you thought at first. It's holding in its jaws a dangling, dripping limb of meat. Attached to the end is an obviously human hand.

The creature senses you and turns. Glowing red eyes pierce the night. You throw your car into a bootleg turn, the kind of skid that spins it around 180 degrees within the width of the road and sends it in the opposite direction, tires screaming. You look in the rear-view mirror. The creature is nowhere to be seen.

You hear a thump on the car roof, and a second later the hellish eyes are glaring at you through the windshield. Three-inch teeth gnash in front of your face. With a crash, your side window explodes, spraying shards of glass all over the car's interior, and a hairy paw reaches in. Razor-sharp talons graze your cheek.

You stomp on the brake pedal with all your strength. Tires shriek. The monster careens forward off your car and lands in a curled-up ball of fur. You shove the accelerator to the floor and nearly succeed in running the thing down, but at the last minute it scrambles off into the woods by the side of the road and disappears with baritone yelps.

You turn back around and drive away from the scene as fast as you can, giving wide berth to the remains of the victim, whom you guess might have been a teenage girl. Several miles down the road, you breathe a sigh of relief that you've escaped whatever that was back there. You fumble for your cell phone and dial 911. As you hold the phone up against your cheek, waiting in vain for a signal, you notice that the claw scratches are starting to burn. Not just sting, but burn like the acid gangsters use to dissolve dead bodies. A smell of sulfur hangs in the air.

"Oh, jeez," you think. "What now?"

But you really don't want to know.

All this could have been avoided if you'd read this book earlier, understood the nature of the beast and known what to expect *When Werewolves Attack.*

## Legends of Man-Beasts

If, as many religious teachers have believed, the body is only the vesture of the soul, some men clearly have souls of beasts.

—Michael Lord, Introduction to The Book of Werewolves

Accounts of shapeshifters—humans who possess (or are possessed by) the power to transform into animals—come from almost every era since humankind first walked the earth. They have been recorded on every continent except Antarctica and, indeed, almost every country of the world.

Werewolves, also known by other names such as "ly-canthrope" (Greek) and "*loup-garou*" (French), are by far the most widespread and well-known species of shape-shifter. They have inspired more tales of horror across the centuries and around the world than almost any other supernatural beings. The genesis of the werewolf is a convoluted and twisting tale. Steeped in folklore, reality and imagination, it is often very difficult to know where one tradition leaves off and another begins. The reports are, many times, a mixture of campfire legends, police reports, newspaper articles, family heritage and religion, all wrapped together in one giant ball of hairy string whose common denominators are fear and blood.

## The Werewolf Transformation

Since the dawn of mankind, werewolves have haunted our imaginations, our family tales, and our police blotters. Do the afflicted really change form? Curiously, this basic fact remains a mystery. Few witnesses have gotten close-enough looks at werewolves in action to register such details, and fewer yet have lived to tell about it. Firsthand accounts of werewolfery have most often come from accused wolf-men themselves, usually during

## WHAT'S IN A NAME?

The term *werewolf* is thought to be a combination of two Old English words—"wulf" or wolf in modern English and "wer" meaning man. An alternate etymology points to the Old English word "weri," meaning "to wear," which could mean wearing a wolf's skin.

The word *lycanthrope*, from the classic Greek "lycos" or wolf and "anthropos" or human being, means "one who possesses the power of magical transformation from human into beast and back again." Modern mental health workers use the term *lycanthropy* to refer to a person's delusion that he or she has this power.

interrogation before their trials. Unfortunately, although the tortures used to loosen tongues in werewolf trials often proved effective in eliciting confessions, they did not ensure truthfulness.

The idea of a complete physical change into a four-legged superwolf may seem preposterous. A more moderate transformation—suddenly sprouting hair in unlikely places and growing fangs and claws—also calls for a stretch of the imagination, but it is more compatible with modern scientific possibilities because it merely exaggerates human anatomy.

It is easier to label evil if it looks like evil. A wolf-like physical appearance may be in the mind of the victim, a witness or the werewolf himself. Hallucination? Madness? Mass hysteria? Maybe, but reports during the Middle Ages, especially, seem to suggest that something different may have been happening.

The purpose of the change into beastly form is ultimately the lust for the blood and flesh of other living beings. In effect, we are speaking of one of the greatest taboos in modern society—cannibalism. In our minds, cannibalism is an unnatural act, and somebody would have to "not be themselves" to be involved in such an atrocity. Yet the Jeffrey Dahmers of the world have done just that, and there are numerous reports of serial killers becoming animalistic and savage in their attacks upon their victims. Many serial killers believed they were possessed by, if not the soul, at least the spirit of an animal while they committed their violent crimes. It usually depended upon their geographic location as to what type of animal would take over the human form.

The term *cannibalism* derives from the name of the West Indian Carib tribe, first documented by the explorer Christopher Columbus. The Carib tribe was alleged to eat others—it remains unclear whether they did indeed do so. However, cannibalism, in all of its bloody glory, is a repulsive and repugnant action that sits heavy in one's subconscious when speaking of werewolves. They are, after all, merely transformed men who will soon change back into human form. But during the time they are in wolf form, they will kill and, in most cases, eat the flesh of humans. No wonder werewolves are anguished personalities. Many times an innocent man is cursed through no fault of his own and is forced to endure this burden. We feel for him and yet are repulsed by him at the same time.

In *The Vampire: His Kith and Kin,* author Montague Summers postulates:

> Primitive people so frequently aligned men and animals in their thinking that it is possible that human flesh was not considered significantly different from other foodstuffs. There is probably no instinctive aversion to eating it; the horror shown by civilized, and by many primitive, peoples was developed by convention, parallel to their aversion to eating other foods considered unorthodox, unclean, or unfit for human consumption,

much as the pig and the dog are unclean for all Semitic peoples. The abhorrence of such foods is an extraordinarily deep emotion, not dictated by biological necessity.

Throughout history, a number of cultures have practiced cannibalism, but they've rarely felt good about it and have often used allegations of cannibalism to demonize others. Embodying one of the darkest aspects of human nature is what makes the werewolf the uncuddly figure that he is. (Well, that and the fact that he doesn't smell all that good.)

Do the afflicted really change form? Can a man become a beast...physically? How do you save yourself from a fate such as this? You do it with knowledge, just the facts...as I *believe* them to be.

## Werewolf Attack Statistics

There are three kinds of lies: lies, damn lies and statistics.
—*MARK TWAIN*

If one is to believe that the genesis of the werewolf is swimming in the dark, convoluted, murky waters of history and folklore, it becomes no clearer in trying to de-

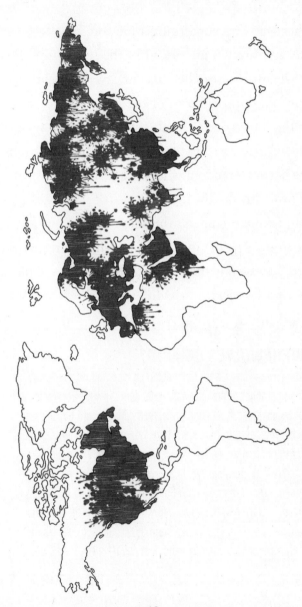

Current regions of werewolf threat based on recorded attacks (1940–2010)

cipher statistics concerning werewolf attacks. So many walls and hurdles are placed in the way of the discerning werewolf researcher that uncovering anything palpable is a miracle. Some of the most obvious problems are: the reluctance of local law enforcement agencies to acknowledge the existence of werewolves; the difference between random wild animal and wolf attacks and werewolf attacks; the repulsiveness of cannibalism in any form; family members who know secrets but are reluctant to divulge any information as it may reflect poorly upon their own heritage; and the willingness to try to see unsolved homicides in a different light. If we hide our

## WEREWOLVES ON ACID?

Many werewolves were rich noblemen who had no worries about being brought to justice. Most defendants in werewolf trials were poor and came from poor homesteads. Many were Gypsies and other immigrants. They knew their fate was sealed as scapegoats for the rich. A staple for poor families was rye bread. Ergot, a fungus that grows on rye, is a powerful hallucinogenic used in modern times to make LSD. Some experts theorize that since most people involved in the mass werewolf hysteria of the 16th century, whether accused or accuser, were poor, much of their testimony may have been tainted by hallucinations from the rye fungus.

heads in the sand concerning the reality of werewolves, we will be forced to go underground to find information on how to protect ourselves. Consider this book the first step on the path to werewolf education.

The best I can hope to supply the reader is a good approximation of the number and frequency of werewolf attacks throughout history. Those numbers vary by region and historical dating and record-keeping. There is also the problem of reporting prior to this age of Internet access and instant information. Things were written down (or not), lost, misread, mistranslated and unsubstantiated. So I merely ask that the reader understand where I am pulling my information from and honor that I am only making the best educated guess I can. Any source that wants to tell you something more definitive is pulling the wolfskin over your eyes.

Rashes of attacks may not entirely be attributed to werewolves. Some of the attacks were wild animals, some were homicides, some were suicides, some were societal ways of dealing with family traumas like infidelity, and some were cover-ups of one sort or another. But many were werewolf slaughters. Superstitious these people may have been, but stupid they weren't. They knew the difference, but in many cases were not allowed to report the attacks in the official records. Much of what we now have is anecdotal, often the product of confessions coerced by torture.

According to one study, from 1800 until 1995 there were 399 solved serial killer incidents in the United States. Of these serial murderers, 337 were male and 62 were female. The gender is important, as when most reports or eyewitness accounts refer to werewolves, they tend to report it as a male. There were 300 international serial killers arrested or recognized during that same period by both genders. So the total number of known serial killers in the world between 1800 and 1995 is 699. However, a study from the Radford University Data Base states that there have been a total of 1,877 serial killers with 1,199 of them being from the United States and 668 of them being international. Obviously the werewolf has been underreported as he paraded about killing people and livestock.

Can those numbers even be close to correct? The number of people a criminal is required to kill to become acknowledged as a serial killer is a minimum of three. Realizing that most serial killers do not stop at three and, in fact, rarely stop unless captured or killed, I decided to use the low number five as my average figure. So that would explain the deaths of fewer than 10,000 people.

Wait! Let's back up a moment. In France, during a 110-year period there were over 30,000 werewolf trials. These people could not have died from serial killers by any stretch of the imagination. This is only one country, not the whole of Europe. Add to this the mind-boggling thought that not every werewolf trial was for a werewolf who killed just one person. The majority were for multiple people's deaths. Let's knock our serial killer mean numbers for these back down from five to three people dead for each killer's output as an average. That's 90,000 citizens, peasants, shopkeepers, stable boys and royalty. That is also in only one country over a hundred years. The obvious hidden agendas and cover-ups that have prevailed for centuries can only cause our brain cells to sizzle in an attempt to put these statistics together.

# CHAPTER 1

# A Brief, Bloodstained History of Werewolves

## The Bond Between Man and Wolf

The power of hiding ourselves from one another is mercifully given, for men are wild beasts, and would devour one another but for this protection.

—*HENRY WARD BEECHER, PROVERBS FROM PLYMOUTH PULPIT*

Anthropologists place humans' first domestication of dogs at between 10,000 and 20,000 years ago. DNA tests have recently established that various domestic and wild dog breeds evolved from four different species of canines, one of them being wolves, some 40,000 years ago. Yet there is evidence that human hunters traveled with wolves much further back—at least 100,000 years ago. Man's superior intelligence and opposable thumbs and wolves' speed and super sense of smell made for an unstoppable hunting team. The dim cultural memory of that ancient bond may be why legends of wolves—the wild ones that did not accept domestication or perhaps simply didn't like the company of men—are so deeply rooted in man's primal subconscious, where fears arise in the dark after midnight.

Ancient man learned a lot from his association with wolves. Wolves knew how to work as a team or pack. They were cunning and deceitful, traits that work well even today in banking and health insurance companies. They were strong, an inspirational example for men in battle. They knew no fear and would fight to the death.

Our brains are still wired with a bit of our animal evolutionary past intact. Some scientists theorize it is in the hypothalamus where our primitive, animal core is housed. Others say it is the pituitary gland that contains a rare, normally dormant thyroid-stimulating hormone called lycantropin. Whatever the hormonal basis, man's cerebral cortex has evolved to be much larger than that of a normal wolf, swelling with the powers of contemplation, imagination, knowledge, analysis and memory. These traits naturally conceal the animal impulses we were born with and allow us to operate as thinking, civilized human beings instead of making moves instinctively the way our forbearers did. Thus the nightmarish tales of werewolves through the ages may reflect our fear of letting our own animal nature run amok. What man did not need was the one extra attribute that came along with being a wolf, the desire for blood—in many cases, human blood.

## Werewolves of Antiquity

Herodotus, the ancient Greek historian, devoted much study to separating myth from fact. Around 450 BC he reported on shamanic practices in the Neuri tribe of Scythia (part of eastern Poland today):

> It seems that the Neuri are sorcerers, if one
> is to believe the Scythians and the Greeks es-
> tablished in Scythis; for each Neurian changes
> himself, once a year, into the form of a wolf, and

he continues in that form for several days, after which he resumes his former shape.

Note that here he is speaking not of a shaman but of an entire tribe of people turning into a pack of werewolves for multiple days, once a year. This may be the earliest reference in written literature of lycanthropy.

In the eighth of his *Ecologues*, written about 35 BC, the famed Roman poet Virgil inscribed the following lines:

With these full oft have I seen Moeris change
To a wolf's form, and hide him in the woods . . .

Apparently, the character of Moeris not only could change shape at will into that of a wolf but did so quite frequently. This is probably the first literary use of shapeshifting.

Four centuries later, around AD 43, the Roman geographer Pomponius Mela substantiated Herodotus' story: "There is a fixed time for each Neurian, at which they change, if they like, into wolves, and back again into their former condition." His comment "if they like" shows that the Neurians were not cursed or under a spell but could change themselves, at a certain time of the year, upon a whim.

Also during the heyday of imperial Rome, the renowned poet and pornographer Ovid reported upon King Lycaon of Arcadia who, to prove his godlike universal knowledge, placed before Zeus a hash made of human flesh. Zeus was not amused and did not care for his own god status to be mocked, so he transformed Lycaon into a wolf:

> In vain he attempted to speak; from that very
> instant
> His jaws were bespluttered with foam, and only
> he thirsted
> His vesture was changed into hair, his limbs
> became crooked;
> A wolf, he retains yet large trace of his ancient
> expression,
> Hoary he is as afore, his countenance rabid,
> His eyes glitter savagely still, the picture of fury.

Around the 2nd century AD, Greek geographer Pausanias wrote about Olympic boxer Damarchus who changed into the shape of a wolf at the sacrifice of Lycaean Zeus in Arcadia. Nine years later he turned back into a man. Although Pausanias had a hard time mustering up belief in this particular folktale and later referred to it as inaccurate, it gave rise to a cult of worshippers that sacrificed at the same temple in the hope of becoming wolves. The legend gave birth to the term *lycanthropy* and also to the association of werewolves with cannibalism. Those who became wolves by sacrificing at the temple of Lycaean Zeus could only become men again by abstaining from eating human flesh for the full nine years.

Another of Rome's greatest literary figures, Gaius Petronius, wrote in *Satyricon* in the late 1st century of a dinner at which guests told supernatural stories about werewolves. This literary appearance of Roman werewolfs, like Virgil's, seems to have been pulled from contemporary lore and life in that era and not made up independently by each author.

By the 7th century, men of learning were already trying to find reasons for the werewolf phenomenon, exploring the possibility that it might be a mental or emotional disorder. Paulua Aegineta, a celebrated surgeon of his time from the Greek island of Aegina, included "melancholic lycanthropia" in his medical encyclopedia. He described animal transformation as a malfunction of the brain, brought about by "humeral imbalances" or hallucinogenic drug use. Though far from our modern concepts of mental illness, it was a giant step beyond the mainstream explanation of his time—"The Devil made me do it."

Around the year 1000, Wulfstan II, Bishop of London, wrote a homily called *Sermo Lupi ad Anglos*, or *Sermon of the Wolf to the English*. It became his most famous work and is still studied by Old English scholars today. In it, he referred to the Devil as a *werewulf*—the first recorded use of the word in English. People so strongly identified Wulfstan with it that many referred to him as Lupus (Latin for wolf). After his death, many people claimed to have experienced miracles at his gravesite, yet the church refused to consider him for sainthood.

## Werewolf Trials

Most of us are familiar with witch trials throughout history as times of extreme cruelty. The church and the government fought for control of the people, and in their zealous drive to mold society into their visions, the value of human life fell by the wayside. Though less well-known, possibly because the era is seldom mentioned in world history classes, the werewolf fever and subsequent trials were driven by the same ignorance and paranoia that created the great witch hunts. In the end, the two were joined by the population's and the churches' common denominator: the Devil. By the time the trials came to a close, countless people had been murdered, and the paranoia that swept Europe began to subside under the weight of science.

Ukranian Prince Vseslav Briacheslavich was rumored to be a werewolf. He is often depicted as a gray wolf. Legend has it that he was born *magically* by his mother, so he had an ulcerated hole in his head. (That must be what a magic birth does to you.) The magicians put a magic bandage around it, which he wore until the day he died. He was a successful and popular military leader, often flying from place to place as if by sorcery. He is also recorded as having taken on the form of a lynx and being a sorcerer. He died in 1101.

Welshman Giraldus Cambrensis was a historian and an archdeacon of Brecon. He traveled extensively in Wales and Ireland and was a great lover of Irish music, although he despised the Irish people in general. His writings were accused of being biased and dishonest, and ridicule was leveled against him for being addicted to the cult of the superstitious and the practice of witchcraft. Much of this criticism was not without basis, because in 1187 he wrote *Of the Prodigies of Our Times, and First of a Wolf Which Conversed with a Priest*. What follows is a brief translation of a few of the passages:

I now proceed to relate some wonderful occurrences which have happened within our time. About three years before the arrival of Earl John in Ireland, it chanced that a priest, who was journeying from Ulster towards Meath, was benighted in a certain wood on the borders of Meath. While, in company with only a young lad, he was watching by a fire which he had kindled under the branches of a spreading tree, lo! a wolf came up to them, and immediately addressed them to this effect: "Rest secure, and be not afraid, for there is no reason you should fear, where no fear is!" The travellers being struck with astonishment and alarm, the wolf added some orthodox words referring to God. The priest then implored him, and adjured him by Almighty God and faith in the Trinity, not to hurt them, but to inform them what creature it was that in the shape of a beast uttered human words. The wolf, after giving catholic replies to all questions, added at last, "There are two of us, a man and a woman, natives of Ossory, who, through the curse of one Natalis, saint and abbot, are compelled every seven years to put off the human form, we assume that of wolves. At the end of the seven years, if they chance to survive, two others being substituted in their places, they return to their country and their former shape. And now, she who is my partner in this visitation lies dangerously sick not inspired by divine charity, to give her the consolations of your priestly office."

At this word the priest followed the wolf trembling, as he led the way to a tree at no great distance, in the hollow of which he beheld a she-wolf, who under that shape was pouring forth human sighs and groans. On seeing the priest, having saluted him with human courtesy, she gave thanks to God, who in this extremity had vouch-safed to visit her with such consolation. She then received from the priest all the rites of the church duly performed, as far as the last communion.

This also she importunately demanded, earnestly supplicating him to complete his good offices by giving her the viaticum. The priest stoutly asserted that he was not provided with it, the he-wolf, who had withdrawn to a short distance, came back and pointed out a small missal-book, containing some consecrated wafers, which the priest carried on his journey, suspended from his neck, under his garment, after the fashion of the country. He then entreated him not to deny them the gift of God, and the aid destined for them by Divine Providence, and, to remove all doubt, using his claw for a hand, he tore off the skin of the she-wolf, from the head down to the navel, folding it back. Thus she immediately presented the form of an old woman. The priest, seeing this, and compelled by his fear more than his reason, gave the communion, the recipient having earnestly implored it, and devoutly partaking of it. Immediately afterwards, the he-wolf rolled back the skin, and fitted it to its original form.

These rites having been duly, rather than rightly, performed, the he-wolf gave them his company during the whole night at their little fire, behaving more like a man than a beast. When morning came, he led them out of the wood, and, leaving the priest to pursue his journey, pointed out to him the direct road for a long distance.

Cambrensis's journals and histories, while bearing a small amount of ambiguous fruit for music scholars on such topics as harmony, leave much more ambiguity for those studying the lycanthrope.

Around the beginning of the 13th century, Countess Yolande (daughter of Baldwin IV, Count of Flanders) commissioned a poem which was written in the form of an episodic roman *d'aventure* and set in Italy. Roman *d'aventures* are written using the elements of magic to play a role in the story line. In this particular case, it is memorable to note that the magic elements involved a werewolf. The countess' poem has not survived, but pieces of the single surviving manuscript of an English poem of the same name written around 1350 still exist and are held at Kings College in Cambridge.

Marie de France composed her twelve Lais (poems) in the early stages of the 13th century. "Bisclavret" is one of those poems and tells an interesting tale of infidelity and lycanthropy. When a Baron's wife wants to be with the knight she loves, she decides to discover where her husband goes many nights. It turns out that he is a werewolf and must strip from his clothes, which he hides in a safe place in the woods, before he can complete his lupine transformation. She discovers the hiding place and steals his clothes, thus debilitating his return transformation into human form. For over a decade he remains in lupine form until he gets an opportunity to kill the knight and retrieve his clothes, wherein he changes back into a human. During the tussle with his wife and the knight, he tears her nose from her face. The legend recounts that she bears daughters afterward who are also missing their noses.

The earliest dates concerning the contradictory and confusing stories of the wolf-boy of Hesse, Germany, are 1304, and quite often that changes to 1344. Sometimes that date is pushed as far ahead as 1744. The tale, which was originally related by Benedictine monks, tells of three boys—two from Hesse and one from Wetterau. Purportedly the first mentioned child, a boy of about three years of age, was taken by the wolves and not recovered until he was seven or eight. The wolves had fed him with meat from the hunts and suckled him. They would surround him with their bodies to keep him warm during the winter. Most probably, he was discovered and brought before the court of Henry, prince (Landgrave) of Hesse to be poked, prodded and observed. If this part is true, it is easy to understand why he preferred the company of wolves to men. If our current tabloids had been published back then, he would have been a cover model.

After the crusades in the Holy Lands, some knightly orders returning to Europe, such as the Cathers and the Knights Templar, imported heretical beliefs that challenged the mainstream Catholic Church. The pope appointed church courts called Inquisitions to eliminate them, which the Inquisitions did quite effectively. But in France, where the Cather influence had been strongest, after the knights had all been slaughtered or forced to flee and hide, the Inquisitioners soon found other "heresies" to occupy their attention. Best known of these was witchcraft.

The written authority for witchcraft trials, the *Malleus Maleficarum* (The Hammer of Witches), was written in Latin by inquisitor Heinrich Kramer and first published in Germany in 1486. The treatise was the judicial casebook of European witch and sorcerer hunts.

Curiously, the *Malleus Maleficarum* rejected the concept of werewolves and other shapeshifters. Kramer wrote:

Here we declare the truth as to whether and how witches transform men into beasts. And it is argued that this is not possible, from the following passage of Episcopus (XXVI, 5): Whoever believes that it is possible for any creature to be changed for the better or for the worse, or to be transformed into any other shape or likeness, except by the Creator Himself, Who made all things, is without doubt an infidel, and worse than a pagan.

The book was condemned by the church because it advocated illegal procedures and beliefs in non-Christian magic, and Kramer himself was denounced by the Inquisition. By declaring Kramer wrong, was the church taking the position that werewolves did exist? Many thought so. Some 80 years later, scholar Johann Weyer wrote in *De praestigus daemonum* that werewolves, witches and vampires did not possess humans, but instead it was Satan who put those thoughts into people's minds so that they believed it was so. He argued that imagination and gullibility made them susceptible to the Devil's influence—and that certainly was a crime under the Inquisition.

No place boasts more or better-documented accounts of werewolves than France, where between 1520 and 1630, over 30,000 werewolf trials were held, almost always resulting in a guilty verdict and a sentence upon the werewolf (*loup-garou* in French) as horrible as the fates of his victims. In a country where the secular laws of the time made no distinction between humans and animals—though they did not apply to nobility—werewolf trials became so popular that they were held on an average of one trial and conviction per day for more than a century, overshadowing the witch problem. Here is a sampling of those cases:

Known in history for nothing except being self-confessed werewolves, Michael Verdun, Pierre Borgot and an accomplice, probably Verdun's wife, were charged with lycanthropy in Besancon, France, in 1521. Under torture, they confessed that years earlier they had stripped naked during a Sabbat of warlocks and anointed themselves with a salve that caused their legs to become hairy and their feet to transform into those of beasts. They roamed the countryside attacking children and adults alike to kill and eat them. They were finally captured when Verdun was wounded while in wolf form after attacking a traveler. The traveler followed the trail back to Verdun's house, where he found him being bathed and his wound cared for by his wife. Convicted, they were burned at the stake.

During his trial, Pierre claimed he had pledged his soul to three demon horsemen years earlier in exchange for helping him save the sheep he was shepherding and this transformation had been the hideous result of that bargain. A beautiful Faustian contract if ever there was one.

In 1573, the small French village of Dole was held hostage by a werewolf serial killer. He targeted only children. Although people kept their kids indoors whenever possible, within only a few months, four children—two boys and two girls—were slaughtered. Their wounds showed both claw and teeth marks. One boy had a leg completely torn from his body. What was worse, the children had been cannibalized. Flesh had been torn from their bellies and thighs and eaten. The villagers knew a werewolf was in their midst.

Bowing to public pressure, the Franche-Comte Province authorities issued an edict on December 3, 1573, that not only permitted but encouraged the citizens to hunt and kill the werewolf responsible. It wasn't long before a reclusive hermit by the name of Gilles Garnier was arrested and brought to trial. He had been spotted by a group of workers with the body of a dead child. At first, in the waning light, he had been mistaken for a wolf, but that was dismissed as an optical illusion of the twilight. During his trial he was reported by over 50 witnesses to have appeared at various times in the form of a wolf. Why they had never come forward until the trial is still a mystery.

During the trial, in which both Garnier and his wife were accused of the killings, he confessed to being a werewolf. He said that when he married, he moved with his wife to the countryside but he could not provide food for the two of them. One night while he was hunting, a ghost appeared to him and offered him an ointment that would change him into a wolf and bring him success as a hunter. Why the unknown specter was being so benevolent was never explained. Gilles chose to stalk and murder children simply because they were the easiest prey to catch.

His first kill was a ten-year-old girl whom he ravaged in a vineyard outside of the town of Dole. He strangled her, stripped her and ate flesh from her limbs. He then removed some of the meatier flesh from her and took it home to his starving wife. Presumably she ate it. A few weeks later he attacked another little girl but fled when interrupted by passersby. The girl was rescued from his clutches but died from her wounds a short time later. Soon afterward he attacked and killed a young boy and ate meat from his belly and hips. He also removed a leg to dine on later with his wife. His last kill was that of the young boy with whom the workers caught him. He was forced to run before he had a chance to eat.

Gilles was burned alive at the stake on January 18, 1574, having been found guilty of the crimes of lycanthropy and witchcraft. No mention of what happened to his wife was reported. His ashes were scattered to the winds so that no resting place would exist.

In another account of a werewolf attack, dating back to 1588, a huntsman at his master's estate in the mountains of Auvergne, France, got in a fight with a werewolf and hacked off one of its paws. The werewolf fled, but the huntsman retrieved the severed hand, put it in a pouch

*Text continued on page 46.*

## LYCANTHROPIC LITERATURE

As the 15th century drew to a close, werewolves all but vanished from Inquisition courtrooms—or perhaps they had been all but exterminated by then. They soon resurfaced in a new kind of book known as the novel, where they have been a staple of Gothic horror ever since.

*Histoires et Contes du Temps Passe* (1697)—The year 1692 brings on one of the first tales of lycanthropy that doesn't involve hunting down and eating humans. A man from Livonia by the name of Theiss claimed to be from a band of werewolves who not only didn't eat humans but couldn't. This may have been due to the shamanic spell cast upon his band. He did say that during the three nights a month in which they were transmuted into spiritual lupine forms that they would travel to Hell, leaving their human forms behind to fight for their fertility rites. Similar versions of this tale have shown up in other were-groups in non-neighboring countries.

Famous French author Charles Perrault is remembered for this collection of fairy tales. Besides the Disney favorites *Cinderella* and *Sleeping Beauty*, he explored werewolflike themes like "Beauty and the Beast" and "Little Red Riding Hood," thus inspiring lycanthrophobic nightmares in a dozen generations of otherwise innocent children.

*Wagner the Were-Wolf* (1857)—Written by popular British author George William MacArthur Reynolds, this is said to be the first werewolf novel written in English. The book tells of a Faustian exchange of youth for werewolfism during the time of the Inquisition.

*The Strange Case of Dr. Jekyll and Mr. Hyde* (1886)—Robert Louis Stevenson updated traditional werewolf themes, blending them with contemporary science, in his best-selling horror novel, still in print after more than a century.

*The Hound of the Baskervilles* (1902)—Sir Arthur Conan Doyle put a logical spin on traditional elements of werewolf legends in his best-known Sherlock Holmes mystery, which has been transformed into movies no fewer than 24 times. His werewolflike "hound from hell" was based on the Irish wolfhound, bigger than a wolf and among the largest dogs ever domesticated.

"From a History of Infantile Neurosis" (1918)—Sigmund Freud chose "the Wolf Man" as a pseudonym to hide the identity of his patient, Russian aristocrat Sergei Pankejeff, in an important case study. Freud picked the name because of a dream Pankejeff had about white wolves in a walnut tree, suggesting to him that the Wolf Man's mental problems came from seeing his parents copulating "doggy style" when he was two years old. Pankejeff remained in therapy for 60 years and wrote his own memoir, *The Wolf Man*.

*The Werewolf of Paris* (1933)—Set in the French Revolution, this novel by American author and screenwriter Guy Endore featured motifs of both Freudianism and Marxism. Although it did not inspire werewolf movies of its era such as *Werewolf of London* (1935) or *The Wolf Man* (1941), it would later be brought to the screen as *Curse of the Werewolf* (1962) and remade as *Legend of the Werewolf* (1975). Endore himself was blackballed from Hollywood as a communist.

and brought it back and show his master. When they opened the pouch, they found instead a female's hand wearing a large golden ring. The master sent the huntsman away with thanks and took the pouch and hand to show his wife. He found her nursing her bandaged arm. Ordered to remove the bandage, she revealed that her hand had been cut off. Under intense pressure from her husband, she confessed to being a werewolf. She was burned alive at the stake a short time later.

The case of madman Peter Stumpp is one of the more sinister in the annals of lycanthropism. In the late 1500s this cannibal killer was found to be responsible for the deaths of goats, lambs, sheep, children, men and women, including two pregnant women and their fetuses. Fourteen children in total was the number to which the Werewolf of Bedburg confessed to killing, not including the unborn. One of the 14 was his own son, whose brains he digested with great relish.

He said he would change into a wolf with the use of a magical belt which he would fasten around himself. The belt had been given to him by the Devil. He was finally apprehended one day when, according to him, the belt accidentally came loose and fell to the ground, turning him back into his human form. He pointed to the spot on the ground where the belt had fallen, but nothing was found. Some say the Devil snatched it back to where it properly belonged. Others say that Peter was just wacky.

He was also said to have an insatiable sexual appetite and had several mistresses, including his own daughter. He even confessed to sex with a succubus sent to him by Satan. Not only was he executed for his deeds, but his two mistresses (his daughter and another woman referred to as his gossip) were executed also. The details of his death were put down in a chapbook by George Bores entitled *The Damnable Life and Death of Stubbe Peeter,* which was published in 1590.

After Stumpp had been imprisoned, the magistrates found out through due examination of the matter that his daughter, Beell Stumpp, and his gossip, Katherine Trompin, were both accessory to various murders committed, and were burned to ashes at the same time and day as Peter, on October 31, 1589. Stumpp's execution was the most brutal: he had his body laid on a wheel, and with red-hot, burning pincers had the flesh pulled off from his bones in several places; after that, his arms and legs were broken with a wooden ax or hatchet; afterward his head was struck from his body, and his carcass was burned to ashes.

In 1598, a vagabond by the name of Jacques Roulet was accused of being a werewolf and murdering a young boy in the countryside of Angers, France. After "examination" he confessed to the crime and was sentenced to death for lycanthropy, murder and cannibalism by the *lieutenant criminel* of Angers. On appeal to the Parliament of Paris, he was instead sent to the insane asylum for two years—probably a less unpleasant fate, but not much.

In the same year, the Werewolf of Chalons, also known as the Demon Tailor, was convicted of crimes so hideous that all the records were destroyed and his real name was lost to history. The offenses included ripping out throats and carving up bodies. The police found barrels filled to the brim with bleached bones in the cellar under his tailor shop. Unrepentant and blaspheming, he was burned to death for his crimes.

Also from 1598, a banner year for werewolf sightings, comes the strange case of the Gandillon family, issued from the Jura Mountains on the French-Swiss border. An enraged mob of peasants seized and murdered a mentally challenged woman by the name of Perrenette

Gandillon. She had been accused of taking on the shape of a wolf and slaying a young boy and girl. Oddly, it was noted that "... the creature had no tail and human hands in place of its front paws," leading some to believe that she had not been a werewolf at all.

To vindicate the mob's action, the authorities arrested her sister Antoinette, her brother Pierre and his son Georges for witchcraft, worshiping the Devil, attending sabots and being werewolves. As proof, the prosecutor presented evidence that the men, while in captivity, barked and howled like wolves. All three were burned alive at the stake. Historians have suggested that they may have been infected by rabies, causing them to act as they did.

In 1603, in rural southwestern France, a 14-year-old boy by the name of Jean Grenier claimed responsibility for the deaths of several young girls in nearby villages. Lacking other suspects, they arrested Jean, who said he had slain and eaten the females while he was in the shape of a wolf. He told the judges that he could assume this shape by applying a magical ointment, though none was ever produced. The judges found that he suffered from lycanthropy induced by demonic possession. He spent the last seven years of his life in an insane asylum, where he died at age 21.

From about this point on one might presume that actual cases of lycanthropy ceased to exist due to the advances in science and industry and the relegation of legends to the fairy-tale category, and the folklore was reduced in importance to horror movies and books. Nothing could be further from the truth, and a few cases of famous modern wolf-men will be focused upon later in this book.

## Becoming the Wolf

> When you dance with the devil, the devil don't change ... the devil changes you.
> —*Max*, 8MM

The werewolf as an allegory is the tale of man's duality. It's the story of his good side, his conscious, fighting a daily battle with the little devil on his other shoulder, the beast. In the era of litigation and not owning up to our own actions, it is much easier to use someone else or something else as an illustration to highlight what is wrong with ourselves. Monsters are perfect scapegoats for that. Nobody cares about a bad monster, and we all

hope he gets his comeuppance. For example, film director George Romero uses zombies as social statements on
a regular basis because nobody has an emotional tie with
a stinky, rotting zombie.

None of us wants to believe that we are responsible
for irresponsible behavior. That is why the most popular
type of monster (usually a male) is one that is cursed
or accidentally transformed. *Beauty and the Beast*, *Phan-
tom of the Opera* and *The Wolfman* are all types of tales
wherein a man acts without rationality and can ultimately blame an outside source for his actions. Even
Dr. Jekyll can blame the beginnings of Mr. Hyde on
chemistry and science.

But for Larry "The Wolfman" Talbot, science and
chemistry had nothing to do with his problem. He was
attacked and bitten by a werewolf (the gypsy Bela who
was cursed with lycanthropy) one night in the woods.
Many legends have it that if one is bitten or clawed by a
werewolf and lives, then he becomes a werewolf also. So
now old Larry is cursed and unable to control the primal
urges that cause werewolves to hunt and kill human beings. In some lore, the transformation only occurs on the
night of the full moon. In others, it happens for multiple

nights every month, usually three. However long the length of time is, the fact remains that the victim suddenly becomes a savage beast who will to do anything to destroy the civilization around him. That is why he is usually pictured as a rich or cultured person prior to the attack so that the transformation from man into beast came be at its most extreme. If he is wounded or killed while in wolf form, legend states that he will be restored into his human form. He may or may not still bear the wound acquired while fighting as a werewolf.

But what other types of reasons could be the cause of this shapeshifting? One of the earliest tales is related by Pliny the Elder in his book *Natural History*, in which he tells of lycanthropy by lottery. Someone is chosen from the village (shout out to Shirley Jackson) and taken to an enchanted marsh or pond. There he strips, hangs his clothes on a nearby tree and swims across the pond. By the time he reaches the opposite shore, he is changed into a wolf. He lopes off to join the wolf pack. He must, for the next nine years, avoid all human contact. After nine years he swims back through the enchanted water and emerges on the original shore in the form of a man whereupon he dons his clothes and rejoins his village.

Herodotus claimed that a tribe called the Neuri were sorcerers and each of them changed into the shape of a wolf, not every month, but just once a year for the period of several days. In his book *A History of Magic*, Eliphas Levi speculated that lycanthropy was actually an act of astral projection by a sleeping man who dreamed of being a wolf. The wolf projection hunts for meat, and if it is wounded while flying about, the sleeping man back at base camp bears the same wound.

Darwin commented upon the idea of a fetus forming a downy lanugo of fine hairs covering its body just prior to birth. When it escapes from the womb, the fetus sheds its skin with hairs and swallows it. Once ingested, it becomes mixed with the baby's internal fluids and becomes part of the meconium which is dropped from its body during its first bowel movement. Some superstitions believe that first layer of hairy skin or fur never leaves the body and in fact is turned inside out upon transformation, becoming the pelt of the werewolf. This would work something like a reversible jacket that covered the entire body.

During the 16th century, the belief in lycanthropy was particularly widespread in Europe. Hundreds, if not thousands, of people who were suspected of being were-wolves were torn open and ripped apart in an effort to find their furry under layers. A mass hysteria ensued between about 1520 and 1630 and the Parliament of Dole in France in 1573 only fueled the flames of fear and ignorance when they ordered an all-out hunt to capture, bind and kill the werewolf or werewolves who infested the district. People used sticks, halbreds, spears, arque-buses, kitchen spits, fireplace pokers or just about any instrument they could get their hands on to detain and rip apart suspected werewolves. Thousands of cases of citizens being torn apart to try and expose the wolf hair on their inside-out skins were recorded. One can only imagine how many murders were never mentioned in the official registers.

In the more learned circles of the Middle Ages and the Renaissance, nobody believed in a physical transfor-mation. Instead, they believed in a mental transforma-tion brought about by the influence of the Devil. As in cartoons, he would sit upon the person's shoulder and whisper things into their ear until they believed they were wolves. The other path to transformation was by magic much like the sorcerers of Neuri. Olaus Magnus wrote that 15th- and 16th-century Norsemen murmured a charm over a goblet of ale and then drank it. The magic took hold and they were mentally transformed into a werewolf. Almost always involving a charm or magical incantation of some sort, the Slavic people of Western

## Werewolves of Merry Olde England

Why is it that in Great Britain there are very few stories of werewolf attacks? Truth be told, it is because the ruling class took werewolves quite seriously. They knew that there were two great threats from werewolves. First was the fear of deaths of innocent people attacked where they lived, traveled or slept. Mass hysteria could sweep through the populace and create panic. Second was the very real threat of rabies. Though the medical basis for rabies was not understood, everyone knew that people infected but not killed by rabid animal bites turned into werewolves; most people had seen it happen before.

In the 10th century, King Edgar ordered that not only the wolf population but also the werewolf population of England be destroyed. His efforts almost succeeded—but not quite. So in 1281, King Edward I again ordered all wolves eradicated, and werewolves, whether they existed or not, began to spread their campaign of fear across the island nation. A massive government hunt succeeded in exterminating wolf and werewolf alike. Stories of werewolf attacks faded from public consciousness for the next three centuries.

Europe smeared a magical ointment over their bodies and then put on a wolf's skin or pelt or even belt
of wolf's fur and magically they were transformed into
werewolves. In almost all cases, a talisman was secured
and a charm was chanted aloud or even sung to complete
the transformation.

The mystery was in how to obtain the charm. The
first people to recognize the need to grasp these qualities
and gain control over them were the witch doctors or
shamans on the tribes and clans. They would chant and
dance and conjure up spells to pull the desired essence
from the wolves and place them in the men to make
them great hunters.

Sometimes they would mix up an ointment or balm
of some sort that they would rub on the person desir-
ing these traits while chanting. Sometimes, at midnight
under a full moon, they would make the person sub-
merge themselves in a wolf pool or pond said to be filled
with magical waters while singing incantations to the
gods asking that the strength and persona of the wolf
enter the client's body.

Interestingly enough, there may have been some
fun with hallucinogens going on, and quite a few of the

ointment and salve recipes still known to us today contain some mighty powerful drugs, the kind of ingredients that would make almost anybody believe that they were just about anyone or anything (shout out to Carlos Castaneda). Some of these drugs and herbs were also found in witches' ointments used to make a person fly. There is no doubt that they did. It doesn't mean anybody actually left the ground though. However, use too great a dosage and cardiac arrest and death would soon follow. Henbane, monkshood and belladonna are just a few of the poisonous ingredients mixed into potions that made people think they had superpowers and were wild animals.

Sometimes, as in the enchantress Circe, the wizards turned their powers onto others and not themselves. Some of these people had the bodies of wolves while having very human heads, and the werewolves of medieval Ireland were entirely in wolf form but remained very human underneath their skin. But no matter how it happens and whether it is physical or mental, there is a transformation of some sort going on. Wolves are not the only things that people transform into, as you shall see.

## Other Were-Creatures in Existence

*Man needs to preserve the beasts because without them we have no humanity; without our humanity we cannot control the beast.*
—D. H. ALTAIR

Much of the fact, folklore and legend of the were-creatures depend upon the geographical location from whence the reports originate. At one time it was widely believed that when a werewolf died it would become a vampire. This created not only another connection between werewolves and vampires but also formed a common belief system that takes into account all forms of shapeshifters. There was also a belief in Greece that both the werewolf and the vampire are of the undead, although the believers of this are few and far between. Vampires are the only one of the folkloric shapeshifters who are actually reanimated dead beings.

In *The Natural History of the Vampire* by Anthony Masters he states:

> The same kind of religious and pagan hysteria surrounds the werewolf myth as surrounds the vampire myth. There is no doubt that the belief was genuine...

In many, many cases believing makes it so. Author Jon Izzard uses the term *therianthrope* as a term to not only describe werewolves, but all shapeshifters who transform between human and animal and back again.

In the 1800s, priests watched graves in Normandy during a werewolf scare, afraid they were going to open up and attack and ravage the countryside in packs. One of the most unusual beliefs was in New Zealand, where lizards were feared because they contained the malignant souls of those who had not received last rites.

Making the ever-popular connection with devils and sorcery, Malaysians, believed that the ghosts of evil wizards entered the bodies of tigers and became were-tigers. Ethiopians held the belief that the King of the Devils rode about on a fire-breathing wolf and was followed by his minions in the form of a pack of wolfs. This was the very thing feared by the Malaysians, and yet these countries are far apart. Did both of these places make up the same story independently or is there a truthful connection here?

There is a Japanese legend of the white werefox named Kitsune (the Japanese word for fox). Seemingly bewitched, she transforms into the shape of a beautiful woman, marries and has children. In the legend, when her husband discovers her secret, he loves her too much to do her harm and she is too beautiful to let go, so she spends her days with him and her nights as a fox.

What was going on with the ancient Egyptians? One would be hard-pressed to believe that lifetimes of toil and building went into creating the Sphinx at Giza to represent a pretend creature. But there is sits, with the body of a lion and the head of a man. Many Egyptian gods represented this duality; the jackal-headed Anubis, the falcon Horus and the crocodile Sobek. Are these pretend fairy tales for adult Egyptians, idle imagination that all of their gods seem to represent the meeting point of man and animal, or a naïve form of show-and-tell? History reveals there is much more to it than just that.

The Navajo Indians of North America had their "skinwalkers" or "tricksters" who are thought of as evil entities and in cahoots with the tribal medicine men. This is yet another example of the sorcery-shapeshifting connection. If you can think of the animal, it has probably its own transformation tales surrounding it including bats, coyotes, turkeys, donkeys, lynx, owls and panthers. There is even a name for transforming into a cow, boanthropy, or a dog, kuanthropy. One of the oddest is the were-*cuy* craze that roared through the small villages of the Peruvian Andes. In the end, the *cuy* were hunted down and the deliciousness of the common guinea pig was discovered from a diet born of fear.

Oucurro Grabling, a professor of geomasonary at the University of Credence in Iceland, is currently studying the strange phenomenon of were-statues. He believes that when giants roamed the earth (a historical truth written about not only in scientific books but religious tomes as well) the shamans would cast a spell on them which literally turned them into stone statues. The Medusa mythology is a lasting remnant of these tales. The purpose of these statues was to stand guard on the coastline and watch for approaching vessels. Professor Grabling believes the heads at Easter Island are actually several of these giants still standing guard. Although the earth has piled up over the centuries and overgrown the statues' bodies up to their necklines, they are ever vigilant, transmitting telepathy messages back to an unknown receptor. There are those that still believe that Stonehenge is actually the leftover ruins of a (for lack of a better term) playpen for young giant children being held captive until they had grown sufficiently to allow them to be put into service.

The list of were-beings is seemingly endless, as are the reports of werewolf attacks throughout history. The background is there, but in most cases I don't think you are going to be attacked by a werecow. However, a werewolf attack is a distinct possibility, more so for some of us than others. My job as a researcher is to provide you with enough information to withstand or elude an attack from a shapeshifter. Let us begin that journey.

# CHAPTER 2

# Getting to Know the Wolf

## Making a Werewolf

The belief in a supernatural source of evil is not necessary; men alone are quite capable of every wickedness.

—*Joseph Conrad*, Under Western Eyes *(1911)*

Exactly how a human becomes a werewolf remains something of a mystery. The presumed cause of lycanthropism differs according to the superstitious, religious and scientific understandings that prevail in different historical eras. The same creature might be viewed as a sorcerer, a

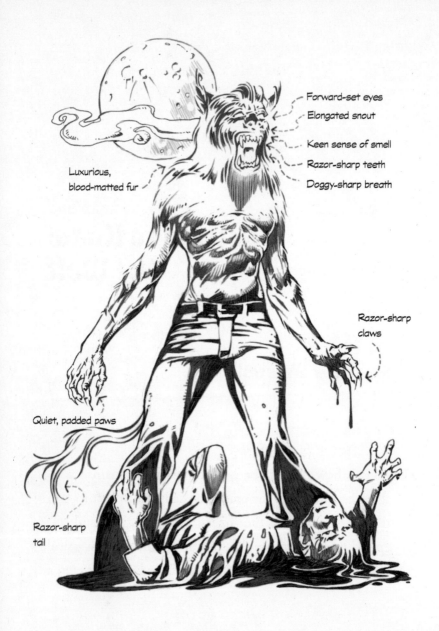

Forward-set eyes

Elongated snout

Keen sense of smell

Razor-sharp teeth

Doggy-sharp breath

Luxurious,
blood-matted fur

Razor-sharp
claws

Quiet, padded paws

Razor-sharp
tail

minion of hell, the victim of a wolf bite, a heretic, a drug addict, a cannibal or a serial killer, depending on the society his human side lives in. There are no reliable witnesses to such matters, including the werewolf himself.

**Magic**    Throughout the ancient world, shamans were the spiritual leaders of many tribal societies. Trained by apprenticeship to older shamans, they often donned actual wolf skins and thus took on the attributes of wolves. In rural areas, shamanic practices persisted through the classic Greek and Roman world, giving rise to historical accounts of ceremonies in which the whole tribe changed into wolves.

**Satanism**    In the 1500s and 1600s, Inquisition theology held that only the Devil could create a werewolf. This was accomplished by using a gift from the Devil himself, such as a belt, an amulet or a magic ointment, given to the neophyte werewolf to seal an agreement. When the werewolf was captured or killed, the Devil would take the object back to prevent its falling into the wrong hands.

**Spells and Curses**    In some parts of Europe, people were thought to be made werewolves by means of a curse cast on them by a sorcerer or witch. Others had the power to transform voluntarily by uttering a spell over a goblet of wine or mead and drinking it—a process similar to the chemical cocktail that Dr. Jekyll used to become Mr. Hyde in a later time when science had replaced magic in human understanding of strange phenomena.

**Astral Projection**   In the 19th century, Western Europe saw a renewed interest in the occult and the rediscovery of "ancient secrets." Some occultists theorized that werewolves were actually humans who had learned the secret of astral projection. Such a man, while sleeping, might dream of being a wolf, projecting his spirit in wolf form to roam the land looking for prey. He would know his nocturnal travels were "real" because, if he were wounded while in wolf form, his body would bear the same wound when he awoke.

**Drug-Induced Hallucinations**   Interest in the occult was accompanied by increasing experimentation with narcotic and hallucinogenic drugs, especially opium, hashish, mandrake and belladonna, which were legal in most Western countries and widely available. Like Dr. Jekyll's potion, these drugs often helped unleash people's inner dark side upon the world. Such drugs may also have been the basis for werewolfry in earlier historical eras, such as when people transformed into wolves with the help of the Devil's ointments.

**Infection**   The most durable explanation of how one becomes a werewolf, and the most common one in present-day werewolf movies (the contemporary equivalent of legends), is that if a werewolf bites you but does not kill you, a virus in the wolf's bodily fluids will change you into a werewolf, too. Modern scientists have verified this theory. They call it rabies.

## The Physical Attributes of a Werewolf

The true sign of intelligence is not knowledge but imagination.
—*Albert Einstein*

Even in his wolf phase, in many cases a werewolf looks the same as you or me. Others may transform completely into wolves, differing from more common wolf breeds only in size and ferocity. Still others manifest as hybrid creatures—hairy-handed gentlemen with fangs and hirsute faces, dressed in business suits. It is unclear whether they are different species of werewolves or merely different stages in the wolf-man's transformation.

For instance, a psychic or mental werewolf experiences the change from human to wolf completely within his brain. He thinks he is a wolf, and therefore he is a wolf, at least in his own perception. He may drool and snarl, bare his teeth, curl his fingers into clawlike contortions, drop to all fours and leap about like a wolf. Psychiatrists see this as a mental illness called lycanthropy. But beware. A werewolf no less dangerous because he looks like a man. He can bite, claw or even kill you during one of these episodes.

There are many folk tales of people being transformed into wolves or other were-animals. In Russia, a drunkard is referred to as a *vlkodlak* (werewolf) because he, in essence, makes a beast of himself. One of the most common themes is that of man transforming himself into an undesirable animal either physically or emotionally. Many women are aware of this unique phenomenon around closing time at the local club ("He's a real dog").

The less enlightened the times the more that mental illnesses were explained away by lycanthropy or being bewitched by a sorcerer or witch. If the common man did not understand what was going on, he would create a story to help organize what he was seeing and making it much easier for him to cope with his lack of understanding.

Certain physical qualities seem to be universal among werewolves:

- Eyes appear bloodshot or glazed
- Hair lengthens or stands out as if from an electrical shock
- Hands and feet appear larger, flattened and hairy, with clawlike nails
- The werewolf may appear taller or bulkier than his friends and family members
- Increased ferocity and strength cause changes in posture and facial expressions

Werewolves who do full transformations to wolf form wear no clothes. The tearing away of clothing symbolizes the rejection of the civilized part of their nature, not to mention that clothes cannot contain the changed body, and even without a complete change of form, the werewolf may just rip his clothes to shreds in a fit of fury or mental instability.

Sometimes werewolves keep a semblance of their human form but crawl upon all fours. An instance of this appears in W. A. F. Browne's 1874 paper "Necrophilism." He describes the cannibalism (an aspect of many werewolf cases) that became widespread in Ireland after Queen Elizabeth burned all the fertile fields, causing a famine:

The miserable poor . . . out of every corner of the woods and glens came creeping forth upon thin hands, for their legs could not bear them, they looked like anatomes of death; they spoke like ghosts crying out of their graves; they did eat the dead carrions; happy when they could find them: yea, they did eat one another soon after; insomuch as the very carcasses they spared not to scrape out of their very graves.

Since cannibalism is the number-one taboo associated with lycanthropy, one can only imagine what some people thought when they saw a pack of humans on all fours eating other human remains. Cannibalism was also the sort of thing that spread the werewolf plague by the actual transmutation of the blood and flesh. Of course, only a century or so later medical research proved that this was actually a way to spread disease.

Put all of these attributes together and it is no longer a case of a mistaken observance by a witness who only caught a quick glance. The evidence becomes overwhelming and the case for real werewolves continues to become stronger.

A major point that needs to be made is that not all shapeshifting is actually a physical transformation. With the many different types of known werewolves in existence and the fact that many retain their human form but readily wear skins and pelts of animals, the importance of the shifting can be found more profoundly within the mind of the transformed individual. But that in no way makes them any less dangerous. If you are unlucky enough to encounter a "mental" werewolf, you are possibly in more danger than if you come across an old-school type, physically transmutated werewolf. For starters, you will recognize the physical werewolf immediately but a psychological stalker can be harder to spot.

## The Physical Abilities of a Werewolf

I know indeed what evil I intend to do,
but stronger than all my afterthoughts is my fury,
fury that brings upon mortals the greatest evils.
—*Euripides, Medea*

While normal wolves tend to hunt in packs, the werewolf has evolved as a solitary creature, a lone wolf who attacks and kills humans and devours their flesh. The werewolf has to be stronger than a normal wolf, which needs the strength of the pack to help bring down prey. The werewolf's strength is enhanced to a supernatural level, far above what is natural. This is combined with incomparable endurance, speed and agility. His strength is such that he can easily rip apart a human being. Those who escape with only claw-mark scars from a lycan-thropic encounter should consider themselves extremely lucky—at least until they start showing signs of becoming werewolves themselves.

The obvious difference between werewolves and regular wolves is size. The principle of conservation of mass dictates that a werewolf must weigh the same in both animal and human form, so a typical werewolf will weigh from 150 to 200 pounds. For comparison, male European and American wolves can grow to as heavy as 80 pounds, although very rare specimens have been found in Alaska weighing 170 pounds and in Russia weighing 190 pounds. One may wonder whether these were normal wolves or werewolves who for some reason failed to revert to human form when shot by hunters.

To survive a werewolf attack is almost impossible. The werewolf's claws, as long and sharp as box-cutting knives, and his razorlike teeth are designed for only two things—ripping flesh and snapping bones as large as a cow's leg like twigs. That is why few first-person accounts from the prey's point of view exist. Most tales of werewolf attacks are related by passersby or groups that have tried to save the attack victims.

The werewolf's ability to run through a pitch-dark forest without plowing into trees is enhanced by his speed. He can move quicker than a cheetah and leap almost baboonlike over rocks and downed logs. His glowing red or yellow orbs can see in the infrared range and serve as a heat-sensing radar system to locate humans and other game by their body heat. His endurance can last the entire time of his three-day moonlit sojourn each month.

Along with his keen eyesight, the werewolf's senses of smell and hearing are enhanced to the point where they can pinpoint the heartbeat of a snake moving underground in a nest, or smell the passage of a human through the woods a month earlier. He lacks in nothing, and should he become injured during his cannibalistic encounters with other living things, he heals rapidly. Even silver, the supposed debilitator of werewolves, only presents a small setback, and he will recover from it if left alone to heal. If you take him down with a silver bullet, do not stick around to admire its results. Get as far from him as humanly possible while he is down. He may recover and return to the fray unless you are able to decapitate him with a silver blade first.

## Werewolf Intelligence

It has yet to be proven that intelligence has any survival value.
—ARTHUR C. CLARKE

The biggest difference between a werewolf and regular wolf is the pack mentality. It actually will help us determine werewolf behavior and how it more closely resembles human behavior than it does wolf behavior.

As with humans, female wolves fight more amongst themselves than do the males. It is one of the reasons that the alpha wolf is usually a female. In werewolf hierarchy there is only one wolf, the lone wolf, and he doesn't have to fight with anybody to be in charge. The lone wolf in a wolf pack is usually the omega wolf. He is at the bottom of the pecking order and catches all the crap the other wolves throw his way. Gradually he becomes fed up with how they are treating him and slips away on his own.

Unlike normal wolves, the werewolf doesn't need the pack mentality or instinct to hunt or live. He can think for himself. Having morphed from a human being into a wolf, although he apparently has no memory of his human life, nor does his human side remember his actions when in wolf form, it is clear that he is does not act out of mere instinct. We are just beginning to discover how much of the human brain retains its ability to think and function as a werewolf brain. Animal behaviorists believe werewolves are much more human in their thinking patterns than they are wolflike. Rationality is present in a werewolf's mind, but it is usually obscured by anger, frenzy and raw bloodlust.

The werewolf is a hybrid of sorts, mixing his wolf instincts with the brain-processing ability of his human self. Do not count on any of this to save you when you are in the clutches of a ravenous beast. There have been cases of lovers being attacked by their former beaus who have transformed into werewolves. If they call out the human's name, there may be a pause of recognition, a moment when the human part of its brain connects some of the cortical islands together, but that pause does not last long. The human who doesn't make his or her escape at precisely that second will be lost forever.

## Hunting Patterns of a Werewolf

Certainly there is no hunting like the hunting of man and those who have hunted armed men long enough and liked it, never really care for anything thereafter.

—ERNEST HEMINGWAY

Werewolves are an amalgam of man and wolf. Certainly their patterns for persuing their prey blend hunting methods of both beings. The werewolf marks his territory with urine and feces, much the same way a wolf does. Although the feces have an appalling stench, it dissipates within a matter of hours until it can only be detected by the most sophisticated of animal olfactory glands. Werewolf urine, on the other hand, is the supreme territorial marking and is toxic.

Feral wolves in the wilderness often subsist on mice and other small rodents, but when the opportunity presents itself, they hunt in packs for large prey. Surrounding a moose or elk is much easier if they attack in a group. The werewolf doesn't need that family support system, as he is large enough to bring down most animals on his own—especially man. He finds his prey by means of his heightened sense of smell and by following the quarry's trail in the woods or snow. Once the werewolf has locked in on what he's after, he is like a guided missile. It is a rare occasion indeed when the victim gets away.

Werewolves need to drink a lot of water. The amount required changes with the size of the prey they have just eaten, the temperature outside, the amount of exertion they expend in hunting down and killing their prey, and

## WEREWOLF WASTE

Werewolves, like most other canine species, mark their territory with urine and feces to warn other werewolves to stay away from their hunting grounds. They also mark as a defense against attack. Their urine can burn the hair off of a dog, and their fresh manure is so pungent that it will stop a man in his tracks. But it dries quickly and almost scentless, so it does not even exist the next morning when the werewolf reverts to human form and bloodhounds start searching for his trail. If you ever come across werewolf feces in the woods, head back in the opposite direction. It would probably be extremely fresh for you to smell it.

In the winter, you can tell whether yellow snow is made by a werewolf by stooping down and sniffing it or scooping some up in your mitten and holding it close to your nose. Werewolf urine has a distinctive smell, like a mix of water chestnut and crushed flax. Once you have familiarized yourself with that odor, you'll never forget it. If you smell that odor, or if you notice that your mitten is beginning to dissolve on your hand, you are in werewolf territory.

possibly each werewolf's individual biological makeup. Urinating to mark their territory also takes it toll. In general, werewolves require about a gallon and a half of water per 12-hour period. So you can figure that a werewolf's hunting grounds will be within a reasonable distance of drinking water.

Once the werewolf has latched on to an intended victim he will usually travel and track downwind from the potential dinner. This keeps the scent of the animal flowing toward him through the air and keeps him on target. It also keeps his own scent away from the prey. Many animals will detect the werewolf if he is upwind from them, causing the herd to bolt. That's another reason man is one of his preferred dinners—the human sense of smell is almost worthless for detecting other animals.

When the actual attack comes, the werewolf usually seizes animal prey by the rump or snout, causing death by blood loss and shock. But in the case of human prey, the attack is most often to the throat or belly, which is ripped out. The human dies of the combination of blood loss and shock, along with asphyxiation because you can't breathe without a windpipe. When, hours later, the werewolf awakens in human form, he often finds meat and blood caked under his nails and his face smeared with the guts of his most recent victim.

## Where You'll Find a Werewolf

Ask, and it shall be given you; Seek, and you shall find;
Knock, and it shall be opened unto you.
—*New Testament, Matthew 7:7*

A werewolf is not likely to come to you. If you're fool-hardy enough to go hunting for a lycanthrope, you will have to seek him out. The quest is not as easy as it might sound at first. There are two major problems in tracking down and finding a werewolf.

One is the limited time frame in which the were-wolf physically walks the earth in his wolf phase. The belief that he involuntarily turns into a wolf three nights a month during the full moon is fairly recent. This phenomenon carries some credibility, since crime statistics bear out the fact that more murders happen during the full moon.

In earlier times, there were various theories about the length of time a werewolf would be in his lupine phase. Sometimes he would be able to change at will and remain in his wolf form for months or even years. This may indicate that lycanthropy can be either "slow-cycling" or "rapid-cycling," much like the mood swings of human bipolar (manic-depressive) psychiatric patients.

Let's assume we are dealing with the type of werewolf that is out and about three nights a month, during the full moon. The next challenge is to locate where he does his hunting. Discerning among reports of bear attacks, wolf attacks, werewolf attacks (rarely reported as such) and other messy deaths at the hands of cannibals or psycho killers can be daunting, if not downright impossible.

Werewolves can live in most environments. Since they spend about 95 percent of their waking hours in human form, it stands to reason that they are most likely to live on the outskirts of a city or town, with easy access to such human conveniences as television, public buses and Wal-Mart stores, not to mention an abundance of potential human prey. Yet a werewolf is more likely to evade detection in the deep wilderness, so some, appalled at their condition, may become hermits, living in remote cabins, mines or caves far from civilization.

There are 32 types of *Canis lupus* in the world, 24 of which are in North America. Some of them are the grey wolf, timber wolf, brown wolf, Rocky Mountain wolf, buffalo wolf, eastern timber wolf and *lobo*. Not only do they have many similar characteristics, but their hunting grounds and living areas overlap. There is interbreeding, and the differences among the types of wolves become harder and harder to discern. This is one of the reasons finding feces and urine marking areas becomes so terribly important.

Also, one should not be too quick to dismiss an entire urban area as a potential hunting ground for werewolves. We have been conditioned by decades of horror movies to assume the wolf only attacks in the deep, dark woods. But since the werewolf is a combination of both the human and the wolf, we should not assume he only stalks where the wolf lives. He stalks where *he* lives. Remember that 95 percent of the time he is a normal human being who must work for a living and find a way to make money to pay rent and buy food. He isn't just sitting around all month waiting for the call of lunar nature so he can transform and begin marauding and attacking helpless victims.

To hunt the werewolf, one must be flexible in outlook. While wolf packs are shrinking or extinct in most areas of the world, werewolf populations are rising at a rate that correlates with the rise in human population. Werewolves are constantly devising new ways of using man's encroachment as the perfect camouflage to conceal their nighttime prowls. There is abundant reason to believe that the werewolf is heading toward his own golden age of strength. He will be one of the most difficult foes humankind has have ever faced—and virtually impossible to eradicate.

**CHAPTER 3**

# Detecting a Werewolf

We gladly feast on those who would subdue us . . . not just pretty words, Fester.
*—Morticia Addams*

Is somebody you know a werewolf? This chapter sets out identification procedures you can use to verify if a certain person is secretly a werewolf. The methods differ depending on whether the suspect has yet to change into a wolf, is in wolf form or has recently transmorphed from a wolf back to a human.

## Detecting While a Human before Changing

When identifying a werewolf while he's in human form, the most obvious and easy-to-use clues are physical ones.

In many cases, they can be observed from a distance, ensuring your safety or at least a head start from an angry lycanthrope.

**Red Hair**  A werewolf is likely to have red hair while in human form. This belief may have been invented by the English during times of trouble with the Irish, yet it seems to remain valid today. Not all red-haired people are werewolves, but many werewolves are red-haired people.

**Eyebrows Joined Just above the Bridge of the Nose**  A unibrow also may indicate werewolfism. Although I do not suggest that the young Brooke Shields, the great artist Frieda Kahalo or *Ugly Betty* star America Ferrera are werewolf material, one never knows, does one?

**Index Finger and Middle Finger Are the Same Length**  Many times the werewolf's prints show this strange abnormality. If a human develops the same anatomical feature, it's a further reason to suspect that all is not as it seems.

**Curved Fingernails**  A wolf's front claws stand out from the pads of the paw in a curved shape. They continue to grow to some length before finally cracking and breaking off. Some humans grow their nails into claws as well and may even paint them blood red.

**Low-Set Ears**   A wolf's ears appear to sit up on the back of his head. The truth is, if you were to configure a wolf's head like a human's, you would see that the ears are actually set low on the skull, toward the top of the neck. A human's ears set at a lower than normal location could be suspicious.

**Pale Skin and Dark, Fatigued Eyes**   Being a werewolf requires a lot of energy, as a wolf's metabolic rate is higher than a human's. Lycanthropy ages an individual prematurely and causes sagging muscle tone. Of course, the same appearance may result from relatives visiting for a week with their small children, so this method is more useful in confirming your suspicions than in identifying a werewolf in the first place.

**Hair or Hair Bristles under the Tongue**   This may be a little more difficult to discover unless you are having an intimate relationship with the suspect. One French kiss should tell you everything you need to know in this department.

**Swinging Stride**   We're not talking about the sloping gait of a great ape. More like Bigfoot emerging from the woods on the far side of the stream, but with rhythm. Werewolves tend to travel on two legs until they need the speed of four legs and they tend to walk in a similar lumbering way in human form, as well.

**Hair Inside the Skin**   In olden times, authorities cut large patches of skin out of the suspected werewolf and flip them over to see if there was hair on the inside. The theory was that werewolves did not shed their skin, but merely flipped it inside out for the transformation, then flipped it back after the carousing was over.

**Born on December 25th**   Humans born on Christmas are much more susceptible to becoming werewolves than those born on any other date.

# Detecting while in Wolf Form

What do you do if you come face-to-face with a wolf and suspect it is a werewolf? How do you make sure it is merely a regular wolf and thus much less likely to devour you? Here are a few hints to help you with such a predicament.

**No or Very Little Tail**   A normal wolf has a large, swishing tail, which he uses as part of his speech patterns and signaling with the pack. As a loner, the werewolf does not need this communication tool. It would be an encumbrance to him. He moves fast, and any spare parts just get in the way.

**Glowing Eyes**    The eyes will often be bloodshot and will appear to glow bright yellow. The glow is actually light reflected from the tapetum lucidum, a reflective layer in the retina of wolves that magnifies dim light to enhance night vision.

**Fear of Silver**    Contrary to popular belief, silver will not kill a werewolf. Well, not unless it is a silver axe blade and you chop their head off. In general, silver is merely small irritant to a fully transformed werewolf. Except … You can change a werewolf back into human form by tapping its forehead three times with a silver knife or sword blade. You can also put holy water on the wolf's head to transform him back. I recommend a squirt gun.

**Taking Three Drops of Blood**    You can also revert a werewolf to human form by drawing blood. For safety reasons, this method is strongly discouraged, but more power to you for trying.

**Calling out the Werewolf's Christian Name Three Times**    This method's advantage is that it allows you to keep your distance. You only have to be in earshot for it to work. The disadvantage is that it doesn't work very well.

**Making the Sign of the Cross on or near the Werewolf**    The "near" part was likely a late addition after way too many do-gooders lost their lives running their fingers across some werewolf's belly fur.

## Detecting While a Human after Changing Back

A person who had transformed into wolf form and has recently changed back may exhibit six major indicators.

**Weakness, Debility and Nervous Depression** These symptoms come from having expended so much physical and mental energy during the wolf phase.

**Craving for Red or Rare Meat** Why not take a suspected friend or family member to a steakhouse? Even if your suspicions are wrong, you'll get a good meal out of it.

**Wounds Sustained as a Werewolf** Lycanthropes who have been injured in wolf form keep their wounds when they return to human form. Check them out for injuries and abrasions.

**Allergy to Wolfsbane** This obscure herb with purple flowers, traditionally used in Europe as a medicine and a poison, can cause a sudden sickness in werewolves. It is not to be confused with *Arnica montana*, a homeopathic pain reliever that is also known as wolfsbane.

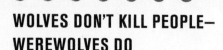

## WOLVES DON'T KILL PEOPLE— WEREWOLVES DO

Scientists and naturalists are constantly explaining that wolf attacks are extremely rare. Yet there is evidence to suggest otherwise. As recently as October 27, 2009, a group of prairie wolves attacked and killed a 19-year-old up-and-coming Canadian singer by the name of Taylor Mitchell, who was hiking solo on a trail in Nova Scotia. She was so close to other people that they heard her screams for help and called the authorities—but it was too late. Could the explanation be that these were no ordinary wolves?

**Dry Tongue and Thirst**   Being a werewolf causes the moisture in the body to be used up quickly. It has to be replenished in large quantities. If the wolf is not doing its nocturnal ramblings near a stream or body of water, it has to replenish its internal water storage quickly once it returns to human form. The person will consume copious amounts of water or just about any liquid. Many a werewolf can be found trying to replenish what they have lost in local bars and taverns that open early in the day.

**Taste for Recently Buried Corpses**   Nobody knows why werewolves in human form indulge in this ghoulish habit, but when they do, it should be easy to spot.

# A Werewolf in the Home: Common Signs

Death is a friend of ours; and he that is not ready to entertain him
is not at home.
—SIR FRANCIS BACON

Many changes take place inside and out of a person who has become a lycanthrope. Some symptoms come on early (maybe even before the person realizes that they are infected), and gradually more and more become evident. Besides the transformation itself, here are some other clues that you are living in close proximity with a werewolf.

**Nocturnal Urinating**   This happens in an almost trance-like state in the beginning, when their human side is fighting with their animalistic side. They really aren't aware of what is happening until they've done it. Then they must go into a frenzied clean-up to prevent detection. Urinating, a form of marking their territory, is the emergence of a powerful wolf instinct. Wolves also tend to urinate on things when they become threatened or are in unfamiliar surroundings. Their urges get stronger as time goes by and the animal side takes over behavior patterns.

**New or Unusual Hair-Growth Patterns**   It should come as no surprise that hairiness is a strong sign of werewolf

## IS WEREWOLF HUNTING BAD KARMA?

The legacy of wolf hunting has less to do with protecting human life than with trophy taking, extermination and blind self-interest. In most of the United States, normal wolves have been killed in such numbers that they stand at the brink of extinction.

The red wolves of the Southeast have so diminished in numbers that inbreeding with dogs and coyotes has left the few survivors with little trace of wolf DNA. The Mexican wolf, or *lobo*, of the American Southwest lives only in zoos' endangered species captive-breeding facilities, while the few who have been reintroduced into the New Mexico wilderness have almost all been shot by ranchers and "sportsmen." The common gray wolf, which was removed from the endangered species list after being reintroduced in Wyoming, Montana and Idaho, has recently been put back on the list.

The slaughter of wolves was not because of any particular danger they posed to humans but because they sometimes preyed on calves or sheep. Ranchers continue to eliminate predators on general principle even though state programs now compensate them for any loss of livestock caused by wolves or coyotes.

infection. With their new "big hair," they will go out of their way to be well-coiffed. They may start wearing gloves and weird shoes or hats for no apparent reason. Pay special attention to these indicators.

The same kind of near-extinction happened with werewolves in 16th-century France, when werewolf hunters were encouraged by the church to eliminate the supernatural scourge. Some 30,000 alleged and self-confessed werewolves were executed, usually by burning them at the stake. Since only about 3,000 confirmed attacks on humans by wolves, were- or otherwise, occurred during that century, clearly many of the "werewolves" who died in the French holocaust were actually innocent outsiders—usually poor, foreign and nomadic.

Werewolf hunters today are reviving the bloodthirsty, horrifying human excesses of the past. Besides the unlikelihood of finding a werewolf, being attacked by one or surviving the encounter, one must question the morality of hunting these magnificent man-beasts to near extinction once again. Think back on how many werewolves you've ever actually encountered in your life, and you'll probably realize that the real thing to fear about werewolves is fear itself, a fear that regrettably leads to killing.

And killing a werewolf can have dire consequences. A dead werewolf quickly shifts back into human form. A naked dead man strapped across the hood of your SUV is hard to explain to highway patrol officers.

**Refusing to Get Medical Help When Sick**   If somebody in your household becomes sick, yet refuses to go to the hospital, there may be cause for further investigation. A blood sample could give away their ghastly secret. They realize they are in grave danger should anybody, ANY-BODY, including siblings find out. Nobody, not even their mom, can discover that they are a werewolf, so they will go to extremes to hide it. You must be vigilant in your investigation.

**Unexplained Absences** Does this person leave the house for a couple of days at a time every month? This could be the smoking gun. Follow them. They may have created a safe "moon room" someplace where they restrain themselves just before transformation to keep the effects of the full moon from forcing them to wreak havoc and murder. They are correct to do everything they can to keep from injuring others, but they need to be cured, not controlled.

**Paranoia** Werewolves may think people are watching or following them (besides you). They may want more home security such as outdoor lighting or security cameras. These poor souls will start to become progressively delusional and develop deep paranoia. As Charles Manson said, "The coyote is the most aware creature there is...because he is completely paranoid."

Always try to be subtle in your investigations. Any indication of what you are doing that filters into the werewolf's already paranoid brain may cause them to cut and run, leaving you with no way to protect the people you love. The suspected werewolf may be alert for missteps from you and others in the household. You must probe this uncomfortable situation with extreme caution and an understated manner. What you don't want to do is create a larger problem with your poking around than the one that already exists.

## Tracking a Werewolf

> There is no den in the wide world to hide a rogue. Commit a crime and the earth is made of glass. Commit a crime, and it seems as if a coat of snow fell on the ground, such as reveals in the woods the track of every partridge, and fox, and squirrel.
> —RALPH WALDO EMERSON

This is not the time to go all Sarah Palin. You can't climb into a helicopter and start blasting a werewolf from the sky as he dashes across the tundra. Werewolves don't travel in packs, making it difficult to track them. Theirs is a combination of wolf/man thinking—the wolf's cunning and the human's intelligence. They are as smart as you and a lot more devious.

A factor that makes tracking them more difficult is that a werewolf is only in the wolf state for a limited time. This may make it much harder for you to bag your trophy werewolf, but it's not impossible. He cannot simply disappear, but his ability to change back into human form may seem like it. You need to address his liabilities instead of his strengths. Each lone wolf is different, and what may be strength for one might, in fact, be a weakness for another. For instance, those who have chosen to be werewolves have a certain control over their transformations that is completely lacking in those who are cursed or forced into this particular lifestyle.

Strikers—men and women who make it their lives' work to hunt down werewolves—charge a hefty fee for their services. If you pig-headedly decide to take your life in your hands by going out on a hunt yourself, at least follow the guidelines the strikers work by. These tips come from years of chasing down human wolves who don't want to be found. Sometimes centuries old, they have been handed down from striker to striker and updated as new technology and lifestyles have emerged over the years.

**Make Sure That You Are after a Werewolf** ...not just some whack job who likes to run around at night creating havoc. Determine what type of werewolf you are chasing. Is it a marauding lone wolf devastating the area with bloody, unprovoked attacks that seem to be as much recreation as a hunt for food? Or is it a cursed human, ashamed of being what he is, yet afraid to go to the authorities or even his own family for help?

In the case of the lone wolf, you have a harder road to go. He will outsmart you every step of the way. If he feels threatened, he will react like a cornered animal and lash out at you in an attempt to escape over your dead body. If you are tracking the angst-ridden, cursed type of werewolf, you may even be so lucky as to have him surrender once he realizes he is being tracked. But don't count on that happening. You will probably have to hunt him down, but the job will be much easier if he is only Joe the Accountant with a wolf's instinct, trying in vain to understand what is happening to him.

**Ascertain Who He Is in His Human Form** If you can do this, you will have made it halfway to capturing him. Frequent some local gathering spots such as coffee shops, diners, libraries and parks to eavesdrop on rumors and gossip for clues to the werewolf's human identity. Speak to local law enforcement officers, schoolteachers and ministers, who usually know when there is trouble in the area. Under no circumstances bring up that you are searching for a werewolf, or you will be the one they begin to look at strangely. They will clam up, and you'll be shut out and ostracized.

**Work in Pairs**  You can cover a lot more ground. Use caution. This could become suspicious to small-town folks. A good cover is as a husband and wife on vacation, enjoying the local color and legends. You'll probably find that the locals love spreading folkloric gossip. Glean every scrap of information you can.

**Adjust Your Hunting Method to Your Locale**  A werewolf at large in the city acts and reacts in an entirely different manner than his country cousin. You should probably start off in the areas you are familiar with. For instance, if you are an urban dweller, you'd probably end up hurting yourself in the deep wilderness, and if the lifestyle you know is rural, the city is fraught with even more perils. Hunt in the terrain you know. Once you become proficient at that, you can expand your own hunting range.

Experience is the best but toughest instructor. A good way to shorten your learning curve is to seek out an elder striker and ask if you can work with him as an apprentice. If he passes his knowledge on to you, such as how to read tracks, you can learn without suffering as many hard knocks along the way.

# CHAPTER 4

# Defending Against a Werewolf

## Werewolf-Proofing Your Home, Car and Business

> The superior man, when resting in safety, does not forget that danger may come. When in a state of security he does forget the possibility of ruin. When all is orderly, he does not forget that disorder may come. Thus his person is not endangered, and his States and all their clans are preserved.
> —*Confucius*

The old saying about closing the barn door after the horse is out also applies to werewolves. You cannot just operate on the defensive and pick up the pieces after the attack. Put up safeguards. Werewolf-proof your home and yourself to discourage the attack ahead of time.

First determine whether you are dealing with a physical werewolf who is under a curse and can't escape his animalistic ways, or a magical werewolf, shamanistic in his creation, self-initiated and out to wreck havoc. If the latter, you'll need magical protection. For now, let's assume you are dealing with a straightforward physical werewolf who can't control his mad, raging binges.

When planning your defensive perimeters, you'll first want a general area fortification and identification zone; this is your first line of defense against a werewolf. Then protect your immediate surroundings and home fortress, including your house, car and business. The last defense zone, if the werewolf breeches the first two layers, is your personal space and your body.

How aware of your surroundings are you? Do you think you notice things fairly well? What color is the awning on the house next door? If you just finished speaking with the boss, what color was his tie? If you just came out of the supermarket, can you tell me which aisle number was the cat food in? We become so used to certain parts of our everyday lives that we forget to pay attention. Our minds are so focused on work or home life or the phone call we're making that we don't really see our surroundings. That is how an attack can happen right in your own backyard. It may be true that most "accidents" happen within 20 miles of home, but remember, that is where we spend 90 percent of our time.

## Staying Alert

Alertness is your absolute number-one defense against werewolf attack. Make no mistake, if you are not aware of your surroundings, you could be dead. One of your best friends is anxiety. Anxiety is a general sense of foreboding, as opposed to fear of a specific threat. It pulls you out of your routine and brings your surroundings to life in vivid color and sound. It's an adrenaline rush. You hear movements around you and see things you never noticed before. Living in a state of high anxiety all the time is neither desirable nor possible, yet it pays to be somewhat aware and a little anxious—it is the same sense that keeps animals alive in the forest and protects mice from cats.

Identifying clues that tell you there is a werewolf present can release the anxiety you carry around with you or heighten it to the point of defense. If you realize that what you feared is actually a mongrel street dog or a bum, your feelings of fear may lessen as your options for dealing with the problem become clearer. But if in your state of anxiety you discover that a werewolf is indeed marauding your neighborhood, alertness allows you to advance to a state of readiness to guard against attack.

Once you have determined that there is a lycanthrope in your immediate area, fortify your living spaces. Much of this can be done inexpensively and with very few parts. Think of the werewolf first as a regular wolf that just exceeds the norm in size, strength and cunning. High fences (preferably electrified), secured entryways, motion detectors and cameras are only a few of the ways to protect yourself from werewolf attack. An even better way is to refrain from actions likely to lure them your way in the first place. Be proactive. Make them hunt someplace other than where you live. Instead of just trying to discourage them from coming your way, you can cunningly point them toward your neighbors or, better yet, the next town.

If you want the werewolf to go away from the block where you live, try scattering some raw meat in another part of the neighborhood early in the evening of full moon nights. Do it quickly from a car, allowing easy escape in case you are spotted by a werewolf or the neighborhood watch. There is no need to leave meat out in the open. Instead, hide it in bushes and alleyways where homeless people are less likely to find it. Once the wolf has marked his territory, he will return there again and again as long as there is food and water. Redirection is better than confrontation.

If none of these tactics works, and you are forced to go one-on-one with the werewolf, training in martial arts is a big plus. Knowing how to defend yourself with nothing more than your hands—as you'll *almost* always have those—can come in handy as the last bastion of defense. In the off chance that you survive the encounter, the story of how you dispatched a werewolf with your bare hands will amaze your friends and impress the opposite sex for years to come.

A large, easily swung object that contains some silver is also a big help. It could be a silver-tipped stick, cane, sword or saber, though you may find that carrying a sword on the street presents legal complications; a cane is better, as long as a silver a saber pulls out of it. If you have a license to carry a handgun, load it with silver bullets.

Remember, a werewolf will return to its human form when it dies. You may have a tough time explaining to the cops that you stabbed this naked guy because he was a werewolf and he attacked you. The laws that apply to humans apply to wolf-men too, no matter what transformative state they were in when you killed them. If the only way you can establish self-defense is by asserting that your adversary was a deadly danger to you because he was in wolf form when he attacked, unless you can present surveillance-camera footage, you're more likely to convince the jury that you're as loony as a bag of monkeys. Unfortunately, insanity defenses hardly ever work.

If you are dealing with a magical werewolf, one that can transform at will, you need to learn how to enter and move about in their shamanic universe. If you live in a large urban area, classes with a knowledgeable Wiccan or local shaman may not be too hard to find. The same holds true if you live near an American Indian reservation or a religious cult outpost. You must deal with your werewolf aggressor on his own turf. If the werewolf is magical, you need to gain the information that allows you to enter that playing field and tilt the situation in your favor.

## Alarm Systems, Animal Traps and Surveillance

One of the simple but genuine pleasures in life is getting up in the morning and hurrying to a mousetrap you set the night before.
—KIN HUBBARD

Since the advent of the computer age, a plethora of security devices have arrived on the market. Not that the old standbys don't work. Some of them are the best protective devices ever invented. But new ideas and technology tends to be more thorough and secure. Here's an overview of some of the items currently available on the market.

Roll-down security doors might work well for your place of work, though they are a bit unsightly for a residence. Rolling shutters are available in a variety of styles and colors. They cover the whole window space (electrically in many cases), and their attractive presence also works as a deterrent to would-be werewolf intruders. Why spend time struggling to get into a house when you can move down the block in search of a less-complicated entrance? Window bars placed inside the layer of glass make it virtually impossible for a rampaging werewolf to force its way into your home. They boast an easy removal feature that can be accomplished only from the inside of the house, allowing an escape route in case of fire.

Although home security cameras really don't do much to save your life from werewolves, videotaped evidence from the recorders can help bolster a court case if you (or your heirs) need to prove in court that the attacker was a lycanthrope and not just a burglar. A camera system should be coupled with motion-detecting lights that come on with the first movement, and electric eye lights for that automatically illuminate the yard when dusk falls.

An alarm system attached to all window and door openings may help frighten a werewolf away. If it has a direct connection to the alarm company, it can get help on its way to your location fast. If the security guard arrives fast enough, the werewolf may be distracted and turn its malevolence against the guard, not you. After all, isn't that what you pay those outrageous alarm fees for? Even higher on the alarm hierarchy, a motion-detector system can come in quite handy if the werewolf uses a point of entry other than the doors and windows, such as an attic skylight.

## Household Items That Can Be Used to Fight Werewolves

Anything sharp or heavy can be used to deter an attack. If the item has silver in it, all the better. Remember not to toss gasoline on a werewolf unless the attack is taking place outside, as your entire house could go up in flames.

Anything you can pick up and throw works in your favor. A lamp can become a sword, a floor lamp is a spear, and pens and pencils are knives. Grab what you can when you can.

If you have that extra second or two, a cigarette lighter and a can of hair spray make a good blowtorch. Certain hair creams, when mixed with chlorine crystals for your swimming pool, can ignite a chemical reaction that creates flames with enough heat to melt light metal.

If you are in your shed or garage, grab a hoe, a rake or a weed trimmer. Think fast. Step out of the traditional weapons box and save your butt from destruction.

As a last resort, hair care products such as hair remover or gel will drive a werewolf to distraction, especially if you can get it in an area he can't reach. Animals have a natural instinct for keeping their fur clean, and a pause to lick it off may possibly give you a few seconds for an escape attempt.

Electrical fencing provides a layer of security at the property line, away from your actual house. When the werewolf touches the fence and the ground at the same time, he gets zapped. The charge can be as light or as lethal as you wish to make it. Just be aware that some jurisdictions have laws concerning the erection of these items as a safety precaution against a child or innocent passerby touching them and being accidentally injured. But be careful where you install it; most electric fences can't distinguish a marauding werewolf from a curious child or a jogger. Some costly computer-based control systems can use face-recognition software to arm the electric fence and other security measures so it will only operate when approached by a werewolf. When their sensors pick up the werewolf's distinctive scent, the security equipment kicks into action.

Homeowners on a limited budget may want to rely on tried-and-true methods from the past such as weaponry and guard dogs. Plant your property with a variety of snares, pits and nets made from a metal cording that can work as defensive line barricades. If you have guard dogs, take precautions so they cannot become entangled or trapped in your various hidden security plants.

# Personal Armor against the Werewolf

The best armor is to keep out of range.

—*Italian proverb*

When the werewolf has broken through all your lines of detection and defense, body armor is *de rigueur*. There are two types of armor—offensive and defensive—and you may have to use both simultaneously.

Defensive armor is weaponry. You have a variety of weapons to choose from, starting with hunting weapons. Any type of projectile serves to give you some distance from the werewolf so that you are not engaged in hand-to-hand combat. All rifles and guns should be equipped with solid silver or silver-laced bullets. While the silver itself may or may not kill the wolf, it will certainly deter him to the point of running away and leave him wounded and easily trackable. If you live in a rural area, you may be able to use hand grenades or a bazooka, leaving nothing to track.

Spears, arrows and crossbows outfitted with silver points will serve the same function but require you to be somewhat closer to your target. Closer yet are attacks with silver-bladed knives, hatchets, axes and swords. According to the legends about silver, you should be able to slow a werewolf down by conking him on the head with a silver-bottomed frying pan, possibly giving you time to retreat. Caution: if you use a spear, make sure there is a cross guard on the shaft near the blade. Otherwise the lycanthrope can run the spear on through himself and move up the shaft to reach you.

Stun batons and stun guns are interesting choices, but fairly ineffective, as your adversary's metamorphosis has given him extra strength and a deeper layer of pain-killing endorphins that react immediately when he is injured. We've all seen film of police officers trying to taser some tweaker and failing miserably because the drugs have left him immune to pain. Multiply that by ten times and you are much closer to what exists inside of a werewolf. Gas pepper sprays and paralyzing gels have much the same ineffectiveness. A flash-ball defense weapon can disorient the werewolf and buy you some time. Be sure to look away when you fire it, or you may have to make your escape while temporarily blind.

Defensive wearable body armor includes bulletproof vests and flak jackets. A werewolf is not likely to spew bullets, but body armor still offers some degree of protection against ripping claws and gnashing teeth. It is designed for anti-stab protection, not a continuous barrage of slicing and dicing. Modern armor breathes well and can be worn well ahead of the actual confrontation.

Hard-knuckle gloves protect your hands as you run through dangerous areas or fight one-on-one with a werewolf, and they give you a stronger punch (some actually have brass knuckles built into them). Some lightweight body suits are made with metal thread, much like a shark-protection suit. They can come in handy for a brief foray against slashing claws. But they are not made to stand up against the ferocity of a werewolf forever and should be used only for quick, unobstructed escapes.

All these protective devices aside, your best offense is not to become engaged in a fight at all. If you decide to work as a striker, though, it is not a matter of whether you will have an engagement with a werewolf, but when! Plan ahead. Do your homework. It may save your life.

# CHAPTER 5

# Making Your Escape

## Where to Go When a Werewolf Attack Is Imminent

> The power of hiding ourselves from one another is mercifully given, for men are wild beasts, and would devour one another but for this protection.
>
> —HENRY WARD BEECHER

The obvious place to go when a werewolf attack is imminent is any place the werewolf is not. But how do you know an attack is imminent? Does the impending transformation involve a family member? Could it even be you? Before you do anything, arrange for your loved ones to be away during the chaos.

The silver lining, as it were, to a werewolf attack compared to, let's say, a zombie attack is the length of time the siege lasts. While zombies attack mindlessly and relentlessly, day and night, until they give up and go away or overpower you and eat your brains, werewolves have about an eight-hour window of nighttime activity and then will retreat to recover from the stress of their predations and the sapping of their energy from the physical change. Unlike zombies, werewolves are sly, cunning, thinking land sharks. They want to feed and drink, and they don't do it nicely.

**No place is safe from werewolves.**   Some are safer than others. Avoid a false sense of security. You don't want to squirrel away in some corner you think the werewolf won't find, only to find yourself trapped when he shows up. One of the lessons the Texans at the Alamo learned was that forts not only keep the aggressors out but also keep the persued locked inside with no place to go.

**Get up the staircase, then destroy it.**   It's best to employ this tactic in somebody else's house, lest you damage your own home. The attack will be over relatively soon, so you don't need the costs or aggravation of a big construction job the following week. If you temporarily block off the stairway in your own house, you can un-block it after the assault. Barricade entrances of all sorts, including windows and crawl spaces upstairs and down. If you can't keep him out completely, force him through a single entrance and cut him off at the pass.

**Don't try to talk him out of it.** In case there is a problem with his olfactory lobes, the sound of your voice will lead him right to you. Hearing you may only enrage him further. The beast may have been your brother-in-law an hour ago, but now he is a killing machine. You need to keep him away. If he knows exactly where you are, you can try that calling-his-name-three-times ploy (see Chapter 3), but don't count on it working all that well.

**Studying up on how to protect yourself is the biggest key to your survival.** Since you know the werewolf's nature, you can adjust your survival skills to combat him. For instance, realizing that his sense of smell is one of his greatest assets, use that knowledge to your advantage. Spray your surroundings and yourself with anything that has a strong scent—air freshener, perfume, hair spray, vinegar or mosquito repellant. The idea is to make your-

## LOOK OUT!

When hunting werewolves, a lookout point is essential. If you were a striker, you would probably have scouted out the area days ahead. But if you're suddenly thrust into an unfamiliar environment, the highest vantage point is best. Locate a good climbing tree and scoot up out of werewolf reach. Use your binoculars, but don't turn on your flashlight, or you'll be spotted from miles around. If you have heat-sensing binoculars, you should be able to spot your quarry and learn what direction to move in. If you are on the run, knowing where the werewolf is may give you a moment to catch your breath, reevaluate your situation and decide what direction to go next.

Use every opportunity you can to relax and catch your breath. Physical exhaustion causes the untrained person to make costly mistakes. Being up in a tree is as close as you'll ever get to a safe zone in the great outdoors. Use it, but always remain on guard. You are never safe as long as it is dark.

self and everything around you smell the same. When he cannot distinguish you from your surroundings, you have a chance.

**If the werewolf is a family member (or you), a safe room is a must.** If you can get the family member there before his metamorphosis, you can lock him in and restrain him all night. Do not open the door or return his calls for help until it is over. He can bamboozle you psychologically into setting him free, especially if he changes because he is under some sort of demon control.

A safe room also works for you; as a last resort, lock yourself in until morning. Many people use old fall-out shelters or basements as safe rooms. Wherever you choose, it must be soundproof and obscure so nobody can find you. Only one other person should know about it so they can come afterward and make sure all is well with you. If you have built your safe room correctly, all the yelling in the world won't summon anyone.

## Werewolf "Safe Zones"

War cannot be avoided; it can only be postponed to the other's advantage.
—*Niccolo Machiavelli*

A safe zone is a place where you can go and not be bothered by whatever is hunting or troubling you. It can be used differently depending on the type of werewolf you are dealing with.

A person who is transformed each month into his lycanthropic alter ego because he was once bitten by a werewolf is basically a raging beast seeking nothing more than to instinctually satisfy his hunger and thirst.

He does not so much act as react, and at the end of the night he collapses exhausted into the place he is drawn to for recovery. As often as possible, his instincts lead him to his "safe zone" before allowing him to transform back into human shape.

If the person has been bewitched into his lycanthropic transmutations, he may be able to think and reason. In the end, though, it does not help him fight off the demons in his soul. In this horrific position, he is aware but unable to stop himself from doing harm and will often create a safe room to prevent himself from escaping and running amok.

The suffocating feeling that being locked in a small safe zone can bring feels like anesthesia awareness during surgery. Too little anesthesia allows patients to wake up, feel pain or simply be aware of what is going on when they should be fully unconscious. Added to the horror of being awake during surgery is the inability to move or communicate. Imagine the extreme terror felt by a patient. Then imagine the same terror when felt by a person under the control of a spell who sees himself rip apart a family member. It's one of the most frightening things that can happen to a person through no fault of their own.

In the case of self-induced werewolves, similar to those created by a shaman for hunting or a war party, the safe zone is for you. These werewolves are aware and able to act upon anything that happens during their time of the transformation. They will mutate into werewolves for a quite specific reason, such as assaulting you . . . you personally. During this time they can think and act with the brain waves of a human and yet are still slaves to the animalistic instincts of the wolf. If you encounter this kind of werewolf, with his cunning and singularity of purpose, there is little you can do except hide or run far from his territory—or barricade yourself in a safe zone of your own.

Your safe zone will depend on what you have available to you. You have more opportunity to hide in an urban setting than a rural one. Basements, attics and buildings made out of cement blocks can all be effective deterrents against an onslaught. The multiplicity of city odors, like cooking aromas, the stench of garbage and the smell of exhaust, helps conceal your whereabouts from the discerning werewolf nose. In the country, your hiding places are more limited. The woods won't do, and the houses and outbuildings on a farm or in the woods tend to be somewhat dilapidated, making it quite easy for a creature with the strength of a werewolf to pull apart walls and doorways and break in. Country smells, in general, are limited to plants and animals, and a human is an easy target to individualize and track.

One of the best safe zones is a moving vehicle that travels faster than the werewolf can. A passenger car comes to mind first, but trucks or vans are also good choices. A motorcycle has the advantage of being both fast and agile for swerving and cutting through tight places. It poses a slight disadvantage in leaving you exposed should the werewolf jump out in front of you and take a swipe at you with his razor claws. Forget bicycles. The werewolf can move faster than you can pedal.

## Surviving and Evading a Werewolf in the Wild

The creative is the place where no one else has ever been. You have to leave the city of your comfort and go into the wilderness of your intuition. What you'll discover will be wonderful. What you'll discover will be yourself.
—ALAN ALDA

In the previous sections of this chapter we have spoken about changing and adapting your environment (whether it is yours or one you've commandeered for this attack) to offer up the best protection and defense against a werewolf attack that you can create. It is the ideal situation when you can construct a *fortress* of some type that will best fit your needs. It is actually the perfect environment if you are being forced to face up to and combat a werewolf.

If you are caught outdoors and a werewolf is chasing you down, here are some things you can do and be aware of to increase your chances of survival in the wild. If you are operating as a striker, there are some preparations you can make that will help. But don't ever think that you'll be on a level playing field outdoors against a werewolf.

Pack this a minimum kit so you can grab it during your escape: Any of the following items are Striker Kit material. If you get caught outside unawares and know an attack might be imminent, any of these items will help swing more advantage points your way.

**Night Vision Binoculars**  Almost all of your werewolf hunting activity will be taking place at night. A werewolf's eyes light up like the flames of hell when you look through these babies.

**Flashlight**  It is especially handy to have one if you find yourself injured in the woods and need to treat the wound. You can also use a flashlight to signal for help. Be aware, though, that the werewolf can see the light quite well. Be careful with the flashlight, and use it sparingly.

**Two Firearms** These are a must. Carry as much ammo as you can, silver if possible. Your main firearm should be a semiautomatic rifle, and your secondary weapon should be an easy-to-carry pistol.

**Knife** It should be silver-bladed and the larger the better. God forbid it may come down to knife fighting.

**Cell Phone** You may need to call for help, possibly a medical evacuation. Make sure your phone battery is fully charged before venturing out. Keep the phone turned off until you absolutely need it. An unexpected ring, even a wrong number, can put your life in jeopardy.

**Canteen** Use it sparingly. The werewolf can smell water and will be attracted by your drinking it if he is within five hundred feet. Do not bring any food. The werewolf can smell that, too, and if it is wrapped up, the noise of unwrapping it will attract the werewolf's attention.

What do you do if you are caught out on a wide open field or plain? For a striker this is a good time to make use of the rifle, especially if it has a night scope sight. Lay flat and use your binoculars. If you sight the werewolf, switch over to your weapon. Remember that he is cunning and could be lying low too. His eyesight without binoculars is as good yours with binoculars. He also has nighttime vision. If you are on the run, take a moment to assess your position and then head for cover as quickly as possible. Do not just start running, hoping to see woods ahead or stumble onto some sort of protection. You are in extreme danger in these surroundings.

Here are some simple, basic rules:

**Stay as hidden as you possibly can.** This is common sense. While moving, strikers do all they can to become invisible. Wear dark clothing. If you are on the run, you probably only need to get through one night of trauma.

**Try to get to a populated area as quickly as possible.** The crowds, lights and noise may keep the werewolf at bay and save your life.

**Use distraction as a method of survival.** The werewolf just needs to attack and eat; he doesn't need to attack and eat *you*. Think of ways to point his interest in other directions.

**Use the high ground to your advantage.** Whether it is a hilltop or a treetop, height equals safety.

**Keep from panicking and keep your head about you.** Do not let fear cause you to stop thinking. Constantly reassess your situation. Listen to your body. If you are becoming exhausted, find a place and a moment to pause. You don't want to make mistakes or hyperventilate. Either one can kill you.

# CHAPTER 6

# Taming Your Werewolf Attacker

## Using Animal-Training Techniques to Befriend, Tame and Employ Your Werewolf

> You become responsible forever for what you have tamed.
> —*Antoine de Saint-Exupéry*

The thought of taming a werewolf or trying to befriend him may seem like a very weird idea at first. A werewolf doesn't seem to have much in common with domestic pets or even wolf-dog hybrids. But this may be some

poor soul, possibly even a family member caught in a curse. Although he may be a killer running amok a few nights a month, the rest of the time he's still good ol' Uncle Bill. Avoiding him on his nights of rampage is surely better than hunting him down and killing him.

What to do if you love this particular werewolf, who may even be the family breadwinner? Well, you could wait a while. Many curses are for a specified length of time, and then the victim recovers. But in the meantime you risk injury and even the deaths of your whole family and half the surrounding neighborhood.

You could try to train the werewolf, or at least alert his human ego, befriend him, and talk him into settling down when he is in his lupine form. This task comes with some unique problems of its own. The first step is a family intervention session to discuss the problem with the shapeshifting victim and get him to realize that everybody, including himself, is at risk. Chances are he already knows that but is at a loss as to what he can do to help himself. Once you have gotten his human alter ego to understand and agree to open up to this training regime, it will always be playing in his subconscious while he is a werewolf, lowering his resistance to training and making the process a little easier.

If, like most werewolves, he is only in his wolf phase three nights in every month, the time constraint is a difficult barrier to overcome. Years of experimentation have shown that the actual act of training can only take place while he is in is in animal form, so with only a few nights available, consistency of training and retaining the knowledge of what he learned at the last session is nigh on impossible.

All the teaching methods you need to use will be hands-on, so you'll want to overcome two things right off the bat: your fear of the werewolf (they can smell it a mile away) and being ripped to shreds before you reach your goal. Here are some techniques to help.

A group of people out there have been working with werewolves in domestic situations for some time. They are called *reverts*. If you can hook up with a group of them, they can help instruct you and provide you with a manual and tools you'll need to get started with your training sessions. Any techniques the reverts show you are there to help increase communication and positive interactions between you and your werewolf.

Many of the problems werewolves face from humans start with misunderstanding, ignorance and fear (known in the trade as "the MIFs"). In most cases you cannot let another human, family or not, become aware of the fact that you have a werewolf in training. If they knew, it could hinder your schooling or even bring it to a screeching halt. People do not understand the special needs of werewolves, and their fear and ignorance can derail whatever positive results you have achieved. If word leaks out, your werewolf could be killed because of the blind hatred most people feel for these creatures.

In the training methods you use, remember that werewolves are best motivated to change their behavior through positive reinforcement. Variety makes positive reinforcement more effective. Mix up your training regime as well as your training schedule, insofar as the werewolf's limited time frame will allow.

**Steady Reinforcement** Use positive reinforcement constantly and repeatedly with new behaviors you are trying to instill in your werewolf. Every time he correctly does what he is commanded to do, reward him with his treats. The preferred treats are ultrajumbo-size dog biscuits dunked in beef grease. Do not use fresh human or animal body parts for treats, or your furry trainee may confuse them with your fingers.

**Variable Reinforcement**   Once you have established a desired behavior, only give treats sporadically. Your werewolf will continue to do what you say even without a treat if you have correctly and strongly ingrained it in him. This stage is also where you can begin to introduce variety into his regime.

**Quotient Reinforcement**   Wean the werewolf off the treats by rewarding him after a certain number of times or a certain time interval. For example, if he is kept in a safe room during his lycanthropic nights but tends to howl a lot, you can use a treat to stop the howling. Later you can use another treat to reward him for an hour of not howling, then an entire night of silence. The same rule applies to any disruptive behavior.

If the training program is approached correctly and evaluated, almost any werewolf can have his or her behavior modified to an acceptable level. Well . . . an acceptable level for a werewolf. No amount of training will turn a werewolf into a house dog. A central purpose of your werewolf training is to gain insight into why he behaves as he does and then figure out effective ways to change that behavior. Observe and learn his basic biology and behavior patterns. The training of a werewolf is not all about his animal side. There is as long a history in the his wolf genes as there are in his human ones. When you combine the two, you go back to the beginning of life on earth. For success in werewolf training, as complete a base of ethological knowledge as you can obtain for both egos of your trainee is a real prerequisite. This basic information concerning the werewolf's abilities and capacities along with their sensory and instinctual

## GRANNY, WHAT A BIG NOSE YOU HAVE!

For werewolves, like other canines, the most powerful sense is smell. Researchers have found that even in domesticated dogs, the sense of smell is 10,000 times as strong as that of humans. Not only that, but the amount of brain cell mass dedicated to interpreting the meaning of what they smell is as large as the part of the human brain that interprets what we see. Consider all the information you receive from your sense of vision, then think how much a dog learns from his nose. If even your pet dog possesses such a formidable superpower, it should come as no surprise that the werewolf's heightened sense of smell defies the imagination.

processes will be used over and over again during the training process.

According to reverts, their training methods can be learned by anyone. So why is one trainer more successful than another? Everything else being equal, it depends on the werewolf. Just like humans, different man-wolves have different learning capacities and personalities. And the intuition of the trainer is also important. Intuition comes from years of teaching and living. The successful trainer must feel out when and where to apply love and where to apply strength. An intuitive trainer must understand and respect the abilities of the werewolf with an almost animal sensibility. Use positive, humane methods to train the werewolf. Like they say, you get more bees with honey than vinegar.

The werewolf must learn what is proper behavior during his animalistic periods. If you don't drill this into his consciousness right away, it will be dangerous for all involved. Always bear in mind that most of the time of the time this is a beloved family member that you are training. If you mistreat him in furry form, he may come out of his three-night moonlit sojourn, assume human form again—and kick the crap out of you.

# Know the Person, Know the Werewolf

The peculiar striations that define someone's personality are too numerous to know, no matter how close the observer. A person we think we know can suddenly become someone else when previously hidden strands of his character are called to the fore by circumstance.

— *Elliot Perlman*, Seven Types of Ambiguity

Werewolf personality has at its base the personality of the human it transformed from. Certainly, as a werewolf he is more aggressive, more instinctual and easier to rile than as a human. Assuming that you've known this person as a friend or family member, you have not only time with him between transformations but also some history with this person and an understanding of how their thoughts and emotions operate. If you start with the human side, you should end up with keen insights into the wolf, too.

Lycanthropic alteration is not just a physical event; it is a huge emotional burden to the human half. People who are already prone to an antisocial lifestyle may actually find liberation in being a werewolf. Behavior training would be impossible with a werewolf who, in their human form, is a sociopath or psychopath. Many of the characteristics of a sociopath would not apply to were-wolf personalities, but many of the human characteristics could not only save you a lot of time trying to rehabilitate a non-regenerative personality but also save your life. If the lycanthropic human you know is promiscuous, unreliable, has a parasitic lifestyle, living off the labors of others but taking the credit for a job well done, is impulsive and lacks empathy, you should have a pretty good idea that you won't be able to control him in werewolf form no matter what you do.

A person who has murderous tendencies is not about to be sweet talked into changing. Although a sociopath may insist that he is willing and able to reform, he is pissing on your leg and telling you it's raining. He thinks it will get you to stop bothering him and leave him alone. He will not change his ways. Instead, he will kill you with no hesitation. Do not mess with this person. The best thing you can do with this person is to bring in a trained striker to handle the potentially messy situation. They know what they are doing along with how to get in and out of situations. Never tackle a psychopathic werewolf on your own. Your family needs you much more alive than dead.

A lycanthrope who has an antisocial personality disorder (ASPD) cannot be rehabilitated from murdering and lusting for blood while in his wolf form. During the werewolf's human phase, a psychiatrist may possibly be able to help, but he will need you to find a way to remove the curse before anything can succeed completely. At the far end of the scale is the psychopath, who has the same empathy that the sociopath has, but it is combined with delight in amoral conduct, which may or may not result in the death of people near to him. Psychopaths are intra-species predators. This particular aspect of their behavior is only magnified when they are a lupine. Death will occur during these times and it could very well be yours, so during these periods, use the evasive tactics I have described earlier. It is much better to stay away from werewolves than it is to get onto their radar, much like the IRS.

At the other end of the spectrum, a werewolf who suffers from anxiety disorder will usually be shy, anxious and tense in his human form. His deep feelings of inadequacy lift when he is in werewolf form, and he may derive strength during those periods. If you can convince him that he is indeed a deserving member of society, you may persuade him to seek treatment.

If the werewolf is afflicted with Emotionally Unstable Personality Disorder (EUPD), he may be consumed with anger and lash out at the slightest provocation. Find a sympathetic psychiatrist who has a history of working with lycanthropy. The anger will manifest itself to a greater degree in wolf form. Even more than most werewolves, he must be kept in a safe room during these times to protect himself and others, including you.

Psychiatrists who treat werewolves don't advertise that fact in the yellow pages. But striker and revert groups have lists of sympathetic doctors who are willing to work on curing your loved one for a price.

## Werewolf Likes and Pet Peeves

I don't have pet peeves, I have whole kennels of irritation.
—WHOOPI GOLDBERG

Different countries have different attitudes about werewolves, correlated to the culture's feelings about wolves in general. In some parts of the world, people believe wolves are the embodiment of evil—demonic creatures set on this earth to perform malevolent acts. Other cultures believe humans are directly descended from wolves, while still others think of various wolf body parts in terms of their medicinal power to cure illnesses.

We can all agree that wolves are wild creatures, shunning captivity and prizing freedom. The werewolf's being is an extension of the wolf's characteristics to the $n$th degree, including the primal urges to ravage and run in complete freedom. In today's society of cramped office cubicles and desks with computer screens as the only access to the outside world, the yearning to run wild and free is stifled, held back, so that we can function within society. In such environments, the werewolf serves as a projection of the human psyche's unfulfilled needs.

Our business practices may also have given birth to the notion that a wolf represents deceit, as expressed in the saying "wolf in sheep's clothing." Many of humankind's maladies are projected upon the wolf. When we look at the evil done by werewolves, we are actually seeing our own evil. But while we hide our terrible thoughts and deeds away, the werewolf wears them on his furry sleeve.

When you investigate a werewolf's dislikes, the result is a straightforward, select list. He dislikes silver, although in and of itself it will not kill him. If he were to lay down upon a vein in a silver mine, he would not die. He may become violently ill and die later of complications from the outrage to his immune system, much the same way humans with AIDS die from pneumonia or heart failure, not directly from the virus but from weakness and inability to resist illness. That's what silver does to the werewolf. But if you forge the silver into a sword blade or a bullet, whatever part of dispatching the werewolf the weapon fails to complete is finished off by the silver, as it causes him to sicken, weaken and eventually die.

A great love of the werewolf is water. He exerts such an enormous amount of energy in his 8- to 12-hour sprint at night that he must constantly replenish the moisture in his body or face collapse from dehydration. This need of his is very useful in tracking him while he is in his lupine form. He can't think his way around this, as it is not only instinctual but driven by a bodily need. He is also famished and will not wander aimlessly in the woods, for his love of meat is equal to, if not greater than, his desire for water.

He does not like illumination, as light hurts the werewolf's eyes and makes it harder for him to visualize things. Even urban werewolves will lurk in dark alleyways and forested walking paths. The only thing that will bring him out into bright light in his wolf form is prey ripe for attack. He will then drag his quarry back into the shadows.

Sirens also are unpleasant to a werewolf. His sensitive ears become painful with any loud noise, and sirens are not only loud but usually last for an extended amount of time. They also sound much like the howls of another wolf, which may invite the wolf to join the howling as a social event or raise his hackles if the werewolf misinterprets it as an invasion of his hunting territory. A small town under siege from a werewolf may be able to repel him by running air-raid sirens. He will naturally head toward quieter areas.

At the end of an evening's rampage, a werewolf will ordinarily make his way back to familiar territory—his human home or safe room—to collapse and convert back into his human form, or he will find an extremely hidden area where he feels somewhat safe to do this. The werewolf would prefer the first option, but it isn't always available to him. That's why there are reports of disoriented naked men being found in the woods or in garden sheds.

To be a powerful and useful striker you must investigate all claims that seem…well, seem out of the ordinary. If you allow the press or local enforcement agencies or even, God forbid, a prominent person's personal press corps to get hold of the story before you do, they will do their very best to obscure the facts and spin the story. Do not allow yourself to become misdirected. Stay the course. Lives could depend upon your detective abilities, so you cannot afford to let up.

# CHAPTER 7

# Werewolf Myth vs. Reality

> There are nights when the wolves are silent and only the
> moon howls.
> —GEORGE CARLIN

**TRUE OR FALSE?** *Werewolves only appear during the full moon.*

The ancient Greeks were the first to notice that the lunar pull at different times affected the tides. They surmised that since the human body is made up mostly of liquids, the moon probably has an effect on humans. The effect of the full moon on werewolves was not generally rec-

ognized until the 19th century. Filmmakers in the 20th century made much of the full moon aspect of werewolfery, which gave them license to use dramatic lighting as a special effect.

The truth is the moon does seem to have an unnatural force that allows individuals who are "slightly off center" to go totally nutty during these times. Hospital wards and police stations are at their busiest during times of the full moon. Scientific studies have shown far-reaching links between human behavior and the cycles of the moon's orbit.

So it seems natural that there would be more werewolf attacks during the time of the full moon, but in all honesty the answer is FALSE. Not all werewolves *only* appear during the full moon.

## TRUE OR FALSE? *Werewolves hunt in packs.*

In popular culture, they do. In Neil Marshall's 2002 film *Dog Soldiers*, a gang of werewolves fight a group of soldiers. In Toby Barlow's 2008 novel *Sharp Teeth*, gangs of werewolves are hit men and drug dealers in Los Angeles. White Wolf Publishing's series Werewolf: The Forsaken is about lupine gangs, and author Patricia Briggs takes it one step further in her novel *Hunting Ground*, in which werewolves control political parties. Werewolves also run in packs through the pages of Stephenie Meyer's Twilight saga.

Most werewolves are loners who mark their territory and guard it relentlessly, but the instinctive wolfish pack mentality can be overpowering. After many years as a loner, the werewolf may seek out the sympathetic companionship of fellow werewolves. An alpha werewolf may populate the pack with beta wolves that he created by biting them. If such a beta wolf never tastes human blood, his curse can be reversed, but only by killing the alpha male.

So the answer is TRUE . . . sometimes.

**TRUE OR FALSE?** *Lycanthropes can only be human-wolf hybrids.*

In the purest sense of the term *lycanthrope*, the answer is TRUE. But when it's used to refer to someone who shifts between the forms of a human and another living being, the answer is FALSE. Kuanthropy is when a person is transmutated into a dog hybrid, and boanthropy is when a person becomes one with a cow. The Native American skinwalkers could turn into any type of animal they wanted merely by adorning themselves with the pelt, but they usually confined themselves to becoming bears, wolfs and coyotes. In South America there are tales of were-jaguars and Mezoamerican jaguar warriors.

Were-hyaenas are notable Ethiopian folklore staples and are even mentioned in *The Book of Werewolves* by Sabine Baring-Gould. In other parts of Africa, one can also encounter were-lions and were-panthers.

There are also animal-to-animal hybrids like the Japanese *tanuk,* or racoon-dog. The Kitsune, from Japanese lore, is a fox who has the characteristics of a human, and actually, the transformation is from fox to human more often than the other way around.

### TRUE OR FALSE? *Lycanthropes are actually descended from demons.*

The answer here is nebulous, as in "sometimes but rarely." There are shapeshifters who are demons traveling sometimes in human form and sometimes in animal form, but these lycanthropes are rare.

**TRUE OR FALSE?** *Lycanthropy is a curse or a communicable disease.*

TRUE…sometimes. Some lycanthrope-philes claim werewolves can carry a "magical" disease that is communicable by touch or bite. Once the disease is transmitted, it can continue to pass on from human to human by airborne contagion or physical contact.

Werewolfism can be transmitted via a curse or a spell. It can last for a period of time or, in some cases, until a set of tasks are completed or until certain skills are acquired. Sometimes the werewolf condition is eternal unless an anticurse of some sort is cast. In such cases, the person antidoting the curse must first discover where and from whom the curse originated and the exact type of curse involved—a painstaking process not for the faint of heart.

**TRUE OR FALSE?** *Silver bullets are the only way to kill a lycanthrope.*

FALSE. A silver bullet works well because of the werewolf's allergic reaction to silver (along with the trauma of being shot). But other weapons are at least as effective, especially those that inflict damage the werewolf cannot heal from. A solid silver sword for beheading will do the job, though it requires getting closer to the beast than you otherwise might want to. Even if it contains no silver, a hand grenade will splatter the entrails of some lupine jerk all over the side of a building. Any method of destruction that involves destroying the brain or removing the heart will kill a werewolf, as will total annihilation such as burning, dismemberment or blowing to smithereens. Some methods create more personal satisfaction for the individual doing the eradication than others. Virtually all of them are messy.

## TRUE OR FALSE? *Hereditary lycanthropy manifests at puberty.*

FALSE. It actually manifests itself at birth. True lycanthropes can only pass their condition on by breeding, not by biting. They also cannot be cured or have their history removed from their DNA, even by a magical spell.

That doesn't mean that we as humans have nothing to fear from this type of werewolf. If a pure-blood male lycanthrope and an uninfected human were to breed, there would be approximately a 50 percent chance of the offspring being a werewolf. But if the child is not born a lycanthrope, it will show no traces of the disease whatsoever. If the mother is the lycanthrope and the father is human, while there is still only a 50 percent chance of the offspring being a werewolf, the child will be able to pass on the disease to others in the normal flesh-tearing way.

**TRUE OR FALSE?** *A lycanthrope will revert to its human form if you throw a piece of iron over its head.*

FALSE and totally absurd. First, it is terribly tough to run while carrying a large hunk of iron, or even a wok. You probably wouldn't be able to sneak up on him while schlepping a slab of metal, either. With the superb senses of a werewolf, he is sure to hear, see or even smell you creeping up on him. And your heavy-lifting grunts and groans may give you away even sooner.

**TRUE OR FALSE?** *You can identify a werewolf by looking at its hands in human form.*

This is TRUE. The index and middle fingers of lycanthropes are always the same length.

**TRUE OR FALSE?** *Werewolves are all descended from King Lycaon of Arcadia.*

FALSE—only the Greek ones are. Ovid related the original tale of Lycaon, the king of Arcadia (an ancient

Greek state) who was reputed to be extremely vicious. Zeus, king of the gods, decided to have a little look see for himself and paid Lycaon a visit. Lycaon, wanting to see whether Zeus was really the great god he claimed to be, ordered a servant killed and his flesh cooked as a feast fit for a king. Zeus knew immediately what was happening. In horror at Lycaon's cannibalism, Zeus turned Lycaon into the first werewolf, which did nothing to improve his personality. There are many tales of people being turned into wolves for nine years after sacrificing at the temple of Lycaean Zeus in Arcadia.

**TRUE OR FALSE?** *Lycanthropes have three forms: humanoid, hybrid (half-animal, half-humanoid) and full animal.*

This is TRUE if you believe the folklore from all the countries around the world where werewolf legends persist. Most werewolf lore doesn't recognize an intermediate man-wolf phase except for a short span of time— during the transformation from man to wolf. There are tales from the woods and mountains of North America about a new breed of lycanthrope called a *liminal*. This particular type of wolflike creature, rooted in American

Indian folklore, first appeared in the mid-1800s, when a captured prisoner escaped from a ceremony in which a shaman was transforming him into a wolf. The fugitive carried with him a curse of living as a half-human, half-wolf—a halfway soul. His descendants are said to be stronger, meaner and more evil than any other type of werewolf. They do not transform, but live their entire lives in a state of incompleteness. Researchers suspect that a lot of the Sasquatch or Bigfoot sightings are actually liminals.

**TRUE OR FALSE?** *When werewolves are in wolf form, they have no tail and retain their human eyes.*

In the European style of werewolf, this is TRUE. However, it does not apply in two main cases, liminals and other were-animals. Liminals can be considered completely transformed in almost any state of the transmutation, meaning they can have any combination of human and wolf attributes. Similarly, other non-wolf were-animals do not necessarily have human eyes and no tail.

**TRUE OR FALSE?** *Holy water and religious icons can keep a werewolf at bay.*

This is absolutely FALSE. Although the church, to control its parishioners, would love for the common people to believe that Christian symbolism can keep evil at bay, it simply isn't true.

**TRUE OR FALSE?** *Seeing a werewolf transform will turn you into a werewolf too.*

FALSE. This belief comes from a story called "The Wendigo" by classic horror writer Algernon Blackwood, but it has no basis in fact beyond the printed page.

**TRUE OR FALSE?** *Touching silver to a lycanthrope's skin causes burns.*

Silver causes discomfort, but actual burns? Well, MAYBE. Opportunities to find out for sure are rare and usually fatal.

**TRUE OR FALSE?** *A lycanthrope retains its superhuman strength while in human form.*

FALSE. A human is a human, and a werewolf is a werewolf. If a creature is totally in one form or the other, he does not retain any of the physical characteristics of the other form, with the exception of his eyes.

**TRUE OR FALSE?** *Werewolves possess superhuman speed, agility and strength and can survive terminal-velocity falls without damage.*

The first part of this statement is TRUE. But when it comes to falling, it actually depends on what the werewolf lands upon. If they fall, reach terminal velocity and drop into bushes, trees or a marshy area, they'll probably walk away from it. But if they land on jagged rocks and are dashed to pieces, that's all she wrote.

**TRUE OR FALSE?** *Wulvers, unlike most lycanthropes, are pacifistic.*

"Wulvers" or "galley trots," are a unique type of werewolf that seems to be confined to Scotland. Their appearance is different from the traditional werewolf in that they have the body of a man and just the head of a wolf. TRUE, he is a pacifist and also quite shy. The Scots believe a wulver appears when a death in the family is imminent.

## TRUE OR FALSE? *Bigfoot is a lycanthrope.*

FALSE. Bigfoot, should he exist, is not a shapeshifter in any way, shape or form. He is just a large, stinky forest dweller with lots of hair. In a one-on-one fight, he wouldn't stand a chance against a true werewolf. I've never heard of an encounter. Maybe he knows better than to give it a try.

## TRUE OR FALSE? *The physical transition from one form to another is agonizingly painful for a werewolf.*

Mostly FALSE, though this idea does make for some great Hollywood scene chewing. The transformation from human to wolf does involve a certain amount of discomfort, especially if the human side neglects to remove his clothing before changing into a wolf. But it is only discomfort, not the agonizing pain shown in modern horror films. The change back to human form usually happens in a state of complete exhaustion and unconscious.

## TRUE OR FALSE? *The moral character of a werewolf in human form dissolves when he changes into wolf form.*

In many cases this is TRUE, in much the same way that drugs or alcohol free up people's inhibitions and allow them to do whatever they want without conscience re-

## HOWLING WOLVES

Like werewolves, the coyotes of the American West live alone—most of the time. On full moon nights, though, when the light is best for hunting, they gather into packs so they can surround and catch prey that would be fast enough to outrun a single coyote, such as rabbits, cats and roadrunners. Coyotes' "howling at the moon" is really a signal so they can find each other in the vastness of the mountains and prairies. Literary accounts sometimes tell of werewolves banding together in packs or joining natural wolf packs. This is the most likely reason their blood-curdling howls can be heard echoing across the moors and mesas before a werewolf attack.

straints to hold them in check. But more often than not, a good person caught under the curse of lycanthropy will still be struggling between his need to kill and feed and his desire to stop himself from this kind of depredation. This is why some experts believe there is a possibility to train and even correct werewolfian behavior.

**TRUE OR FALSE?** *Mistletoe, rye and wolfsbane ward off werewolves.*

TRUE, because they hate either the smell or the taste, but there is nothing magical concerning any of these plants and their effects upon a werewolf.

**TRUE OR FALSE?** *Werewolves can change shape at will.*

TRUE for some types of werewolves, but not all.

**TRUE OR FALSE?** *Werewolves must consume raw meat in order to survive.*

TRUE, though it need not be human meat. Cattle, sheep, dogs or just about anything living will suffice to quaff their need for blood and meat. Eating only nonhuman flesh is one of the few things werewolves can do to avoid the wrenching guilt their human side may feel about being serial murderers. It has gotten many a werewolf through the hard times until a cure was found to relieve them of their problem.

**TRUE OR FALSE?** *Mercury (quicksilver) will harm or kill a werewolf.*

Absolutely TRUE. And also your children, your chemistry teacher and the guy who works at the thermometer factory. Mercury is a deadly poison, and even touching it over a period of time will cause dementia, hence the term "mad as a hatter"—men's hat makers used to use mercury to polish hats.

**TRUE OR FALSE?** *A child conceived on the night of a new moon will become a werewolf.*

FALSE. This old Sicilian legend bears no semblance of truth. If it were true, there would be a lot more werewolves running amok in this world. A similar Romanian folktale holds that a child conceived on Easter or Christmas Day will be a werewolf, which is also false.

**TRUE OR FALSE?** *The seventh consecutive son in a family will become a werewolf.*

Several variations of this fable exist. According to one, the seventh consecutive son in a family will become a werewolf from midnight to 2:00 a.m. every night starting on his thirteenth birthday. All these seventh-son stories are FALSE.

**TRUE OR FALSE?** *A flower found in the Balkans, when worn in the lapel or hatband, will transform the wearer into a werewolf.*

FALSE. This tale may have originated with a grumpy old lady who wanted to scare away kids from picking her flowers. On the other hand, there's rumored to be a flower in eastern Europe that has the power to transform you into a grumpy old lady.

# CHAPTER 8

# Modern Werewolf Legends

Authenticity matters little, though—our willingness to accept legends depends far more upon their expression of concepts we want to believe than upon their plausibility.

—*DAVID P. MIKKELSON, SNOPES.COM*

Werewolf tales are a lot like ghost stories. Not everybody has seen a werewolf, but everybody knows somebody who has seen one or has a friend, cousin or neighbor who has seen one. The term for that is a FOAF (Friend of a Friend). This is the unimpeachable eyewitness nobody can produce. "I heard about this guy who used to come into the store where my nephew works ..." Some-

times the story is real, and sometimes it isn't, but you can never fully verify the circumstances. You have to take the evidence at face value and decide for yourself.

As with Santa Claus, you cannot disprove the existence of werewolves. You can only prove or disprove a particular instance. That's why these tales never die but instead live on in the imaginations of the tellers and listeners around a campfire, a local bar or a family gathering. The truth is, we *want* them to exist. They prove that man does not have total control over our world, and when we lose our way in life, it's just because we are human and don't know everything.

Here are a few of the present-day urban legends, small-town rumors and Internet factoids in circulation.

In 1975 the Robson family of Hexham, England, discovered what appeared to be two Celtic stone heads in their garden. Mrs. Robson and the neighbor brought the pair inside and cleaned them off, trying without success to ascertain their origin. The heads were quite a source of interest around the little burg, and they decided to locate an expert in Celtic mythology to see what further information they could obtain. The heads were set aside for later investigation, and life resumed its normal pace.

According to a report on the BBC current affairs program *Nationwide*, Mrs. Robson was startled awake by loud smashing and banging coming from her neighbor's house. It soon stopped and she went back to sleep.

The following day, the neighbor claimed she had been tucking her daughter into bed when she glanced up and saw a creature "like a werewolf" go past the door to the room. Half-human, half-animal, the creature shocked her. She screamed, and her husband came running out of his room in time to hear something large running down the steps and breaking through the front door (the crashing Mrs. Robson had heard).

But it didn't end there. Trouble seemed to follow the stone heads and whoever had handled them. The artifacts were sent to Dr. Anne Ross, an expert in Celtic mythology in Southhampton, who also found them intriguing. Soon afterward, a noise awakened her one night in time to observe a large black shape against the inside of the white door of her house. It was at least six feet in height, covered in fur and slightly stooped. In the doctor's words, "It was half-animal and half-man. The upper part was a wolf and the lower part was human." The beast ran outside and disappeared into the night.

Was it true? What was the creature after? What secret did the stones heads hold? Were they responsible for summoning the beast? We may never know; but the fact that the story was broadcast gave it an even greater aura of authenticity. It must have been true if it was on the radio. Such is the power of the modern media.

Wittlich, Germany, has a key role in the history of werewolves. If tales be told correctly, it is the reported site of the last werewolf killed in Germany. There is a shrine with an eternal flame at a location on the edge of town. Word of mouth has it that if the flame is ever extinguished, the werewolves will return.

On a cold night in 1988, policemen were on their way back to their posts at the Morback Munitions Base when they noticed that the flame was out. They laughed and joked among themselves about being extra careful so as not to get attacked by a werewolf. A few hours later, the alarms sounded, indicating that the perimeter fence had been unlawfully breached.

Several military men came running to the scene of the breach. There they witnessed a wolflike animal seven to eight feet tall on its hind legs. The guard dog reportedly went crazy upon seeing it but would not follow or attack the creature. After snarling loudly, the beast took three long leaping steps, jumped over the 12-foot-tall security fence and disappeared into the darkness. The guards had been too stunned to shoot at it or even radio for backup. It all happened too quickly. Why was it there? And just exactly what was it, anyway? The flame was relit soon after, and no further sightings have been reported.

European sightings have a long and varied history, but North America is no slouch when it comes to werewolf-sightings either. For instance, the lycanthrope tradition endures in the Louisiana bayous with the Cajun tales of the *rougarou* or *loup-garou*. Many ancestors of the Cajuns came from France not long after the werewolf hysteria of the 16th century, and other tales of the supernatural have been slithering out of the backwoods and swamps ever since.

The creature said to roam the southern Louisiana wilderness is said to attack and kill Catholics who have not followed the rules of Lent. One way to transform into a werewolf, at least in Louisiana, is to break Lent seven years in a row.

Tales of people who fall under the werewolf curse after having their blood sucked at night are common in

Cajun communities. The bloodsucker is depicted as having a human body with a wolf head.

In the southwestern United States during the year 1973, there were a number of reported sightings of a fur-covered, wolflike creature that stood on two feet. It was said to be seven to eight feet tall, with red eyes that either glowed in the darkness or acted like reflectors, using the light from streetlights and flashlights. Descriptions almost exactly match those given for the fugitive creature seen at the munitions dump in Germany. Of course, among the Navajo, some people that Western psychiatrists would characterize as sociopaths become "skinwalkers," recluses who wear wolf skins to transform themselves and roam the night doing evil deeds.

The United States is not alone in these scattered reports of strange creatures. The chupacabra of Mexico appears to be a cousin of the werewolf and, for that matter, the vampire. Though probably no threat to man, this hairy beast is said to suck all the blood from goats, and in New Mexico and southern Colorado it is a "creature of interest" in the mysterious waves of cattle mutilations that happen from time to time.

Around 1980 in Dauphin, Manitoba, a large group of high school kids decided to use an abandoned farmhouse as the location of their next big party. It was perfect, somewhat isolated, so their music and noisemaking wouldn't be heard by neighbors. Even better, the house had been abandoned completely furnished.

That night, the group of more than 100 kids descended upon the house and the festivities began. One small group of jocks decided to pry open the cellar door to check out what might be down there. Hoping for a cache of liquor, they busted it open. Suddenly the walls began to shake, and there was a loud stomping from something coming up the stairs toward the party. Everyone started screaming and running from the house. Some people jumped right through the living room window. A beast described as eight to nine feet tall and covered with fur emerged from the cellar. It stood on two feet and had the head of a wolf, but slightly wider, and with pointed ears. It reached down and tore the center kitchen island from the floor and flung it aside. In its fury it ripped cabinets from off the walls before smashing through the back door and out into the night. It was never seen again. Luckily, no one sustained injuries, except for posttraumatic stress disorder from the fright.

In Kentucky, they have tales not only of werewolves but also of their offspring. A report from Pikeville tells of a homeowner who kept hearing noises out on his porch. He lived outside of town in a rural area, so he thought it was probably a deer or a raccoon. He went to the screen door and flipped on the porch light. Looking back at him was what appeared to be a hairy child whose face was that of a dog. They stared at each other for a few moments; then the boy turned and left. Evidently he had been foraging for food.

As you head west toward chaparral country, the stories continue to mount. A couple who lived just outside of Dallas was traveling to Austin with their two big dogs in tow. It was night when they stopped to gas up their SUV. They had finished fueling and headed back onto the highway when they became disorientated and ended up on the dirt service road that paralleled the highway. Assuming it would eventually take them to the next highway entrance, they continued on. Suddenly the dogs began barking excitedly and jumping around in the car.

Thinking that the dogs might need to relieve themselves, the husband pulled over and went around to open the side door. The dogs would not get out, but remained inside the SUV growling.

Looking over at the fence that separated the road from the woods, they saw what appeared to be a tall, heavyset man with a rather large head. He was eating something that he held in his hands. He wore no shirt and was covered with hair, slurping loudly and ferociously while devouring his meal. When he looked up at the people near the car, they could see that his eyes glowed red. The husband jumped into the side door and pulled it shut behind him, yelling at his wife to lock the doors. The man-beast watched them for a second and then jumped over a fence and ran into the woods. Shaken, they drove away with the dogs barking the whole way. To this day they still don't know if it was a werewolf or a feral prairie man of some type, but they have never forgotten that night.

In Gallup, New Mexico, in January of 1970, four teenagers reported coming upon a werewolf alongside the road. It could have been a skinwalker, since the Navajo Nation owns most of the ranchland around Gallup.

But this creature kept pace with their car at speeds of over 60 mph, much faster than a human can run even with magical powers, until one of the boys shot the creature. It let out a shriek and ran off into the underbrush.

Around 1998 in Albuquerque, New Mexico, a young man at a campsite was awaiting the return of his friends when he saw what he claimed to be a skinwalker. At first he thought it was a coyote walking upright. But since coyotes walk on all four legs, he quickly dismissed that idea. The beast appeared to move with great ease and fluidity on two legs, and for a brief moment it looked a lot like a middle-aged Indian. Without ever pausing to confront the kid, it walked down into an arroyo and disappeared into the darkness. The frightened boy turned and hauled his butt back to the vehicles.

In 1994, an unknowing family named Sherman bought a 480-acre ranch in western Utah on the edge of the Ute reservation. Within two years they were forced off the land by the extreme amounts of paranormal activity taking place there. Huge wolflike creatures that seemed impervious to gunshots would attack their livestock and horses. A variety of other strange creatures would appear, from Bigfoot-type mammals to exotically colored birds and fowl. Lights could be seen shining upward out the ground. They claimed that sometimes the area was lit up like a high school football field at night. Huge chunks of earth precisely excavated in concentric circles like British cop circles would be found in the morning.

It wasn't just the Sherman Ranch that was having this activity. It seemed to be happening throughout the Unitah Basin where the ranch was located. It unnerved the family so much that in 1996 they decided to sell the property and get out while the gettin' was good. The locals and the press came to refer to the place as Skinwalker Ranch.

Nobody was interested in buying the place until the National Institute for Discovery Science took notice of it and shelled out $200,000 for it. George Knapp of the *Las Vegas Mercury* wrote a book about the place in 2002, detailing all of the strange goings-on, including glowing blue orbs, disembodied voices and UFOs. Cattle mutilations had been common there since at least the 1960s. Some say it was cursed by the Ute Indians, who sent skinwalkers as messengers of that curse.

One of the oddest sightings happened in Mobile, Alabama, in the early spring of 1971, when a neighborhood rose up in arms over nighttime meetings with a strange creature. One witness claimed, "The top half was a woman and the bottom was a wolf." Female werewolves are quite unusual—so much so that another witness added, "It didn't seem natural." The city of Mobile Police Department investigated the reports. The final results were inconclusive.

In 1997, just outside of Asheville, North Carolina, a young man pushed his four-cylinder Toyota hard, trying to conquer the central mountains along Interstate 40. It was dark and rainy, and the little car chugged on. Soon it began to overheat and slow down as the driver forced it up the steep grades. Rounding a curve, his headlights flashed on an amazing sight. A werewolf was sitting squat on the side of the highway devouring a deer. It looked up with angered red eyes glowing as the headlights flashed on it. It grabbed a hunk of the deer and jumped into the bushes at the side of the road.

Three years later, a young man was spending time at his mother's home in Kentucky. An experienced woodsman and hunter, he had seen his share of unique tracks and creepy scat in the forests. He was sound asleep when his mother awoke him around midnight. She said she was hearing noises from the backyard and splashing in the creek. Still half-asleep, he followed his mother downstairs to the ground floor. As they listened, they could hear two or three animals growling, grunting and splashing in the creek.

There had been bear sightings in the area. But the cries that were coming from the creek were not those of a baby bear or its mother. They were somewhat wolfish but ethereal at the same time. Their volume carried throughout the woods. Suddenly the splashing stopped, and the sound of animals walking could be heard as they traveled off toward the mountain range behind the house. The next morning there were no footprints in the soft creekside sand and no other traces that the tracker could spot.

Generally speaking, the Midwestern United States seems to have a band of werewolf activity from Kentucky to Lake Michigan. In northwestern Ohio, Allen County and its main towns, Defiance and Delphos, are the heart of the Great Black Swamp. The swamp has been mostly drained, and now lush farms dot the countryside. The Auglaize River runs through it, and it has come to be known as prime werewolf habitat. In fact, Ohio has the fourth-largest number of werewolf sighting reports out of all the states in the U.S. (The other three states are in the Pacific Northwest.) Werewolf sightings are so common that the police in the area take them very seriously.

The Arlington, Ohio, area has also had quite a few reports of werewolf activity. In one instance, a couple of guys saw what at first appeared to be a large dog running along the side of the road. When it began to cross in front of them, they stopped the car. The animal turned to face the vehicle and thumped the hood with its paws. It was longer and much fuller than a dog.

There were also reports of a beast that was too tall and slender to be a bear running about in the farmlands. Never captured, the beast may still be roaming at large to this day. Ohio's antipoaching law prohibits killing such beasts, even if you were only to bring in a single paw or ear as evidence of the sighting. So if any werewolves have been killed, the hunters are keeping it quiet.

Farther to the north, tales persist of the famed Michigan Dog Man. The centerpiece of those speculations is a shaky 8mm film that shows people snowmobiling. In the last few seconds of the film, the "dog man" shows up on all fours and moves at a quick clip toward the camera, which spins as if the videographer is turning and running. The running stops, and we get a last glimpse of the field sans dog man. Suddenly jaws, teeth and a gaping animal mouth fill the screen, and the camera drops to the ground.

It would have to be a very athletic human indeed to move in the manner of the dog man. He sidles at a quick rate of speed on all fours. He has ears high up on his head, not at all like a dog or bear. The film is disturbing in its lack of graphic finale, unlike many of the "companion" pieces that have since surfaced purporting to contain more of the same.

Many sightings have occurred in the Reed City area of Michigan's lower peninsula, the hotbed of dog man activity, as recently as 2006. Descriptions put them between six-and-a-half and seven feet tall, covered in long dark brown or black hair. They are slender, not at all like Bigfoot descriptions, and their weight is estimated at 200 to 230 pounds. Their arms hang lower than humans', and they stand a bit hunched over. They appear to be able to move efficiently on either two legs or four. The eyes are angled and yellowish, although this could be due to photographers' lights reflecting from the beasts' retinas, as most of the sightings take place at night. That is another of the unusual things about the original dog man film: it takes place in total daylight. The beasts seem to have narrow snouts, but not long or wolfish, more like halfway between human and dog, with broad foreheads. They seem to populate swampy areas of the countryside, though there is nothing aquatic about their appearance.

In 1986 a young soldier who had been brought up as an outdoorsman left the Manistee, Michigan, Army Recruiting Station where he worked and headed home to Ludington. It was autumn, and the darkness had already fallen. In that largely rural area, the deer graze freely and drivers on the two-lane blacktop roads have to be vigilant so as not to hit one. As he rounded one corner, he saw a pair of yellow eyes reflecting his headlights from a farm field. It troubled him that the eyes, which were all he could see, were too high and too far apart to be a deer. It might have been some type of bear—or, at that height, maybe a moose. The soldier was six-feet-two-inches tall, and he estimated that the animal was much taller than he was.

The animal continued to stare at him and move at the same time. The darkened shape ran across the field and jumped while continuing to stare at him. It jumped three times, and the leaps were far larger than any animal he knew of. Moose and bear were ruled out. Its final leap crossed in front of his car, completely clearing the full width of the two-lane road, and it dashed off into the woods on the other side. We'll never know if this was a dog man of Michigan or not.

One of the most famous stories takes place in Wisconsin. There have been many news reports and books written about the most famous of all American werewolves—the Beast of Bray Road. But this heartland state's reputation goes back far earlier than the Bray Road incidents. Back in 1936, the first detailed incident was reported by Mark Shackelman, who spoke of seeing a wolf-man while driving down Highway 18. Sightings persisted, most notably in 1964 and 1972, and then the scat hit the fan in 1989, continuing through 1992, near Delavan, Wisconsin. The cases have yet to be solved.

A young married woman, a native of Walworth County, sighted an amazing figure one day while sitting on her back porch. She described it as looking like "a starved Bigfoot with a wolfish face." She went on to describe the too-long arms that swung and turned in an almost buglike fashion. The beast had a height of nearly seven feet. She said that about a month before the sighting occurred, deer had stopped coming into their backyard.

In 1989 Lorianne Endrizzi, a 24-year-old bar manager, was driving home when she spotted what she took to be a man hunched over at the side of the road. As she came upon the figure, she slowed down, and he turned and looked at her from the passenger side of the road. It was a wolfish beast with gray-brown hair, fangs and pointed ears. He had a long snout like a wolf. Even though the headlights were not directly on the beast, its eyes glowed yellow in the night. It used its extended arms like a human, holding its food palm-upward as it ate. The chest seemed wide and barrel-like. She had no idea what this unnerving sight had been until she later came upon a picture of a werewolf and gasped with recognition.

She contacted the Lakeland Animal Shelter about the incident and was told by county humane officer John Frederickson that quite a few other people also had reported seeing something unusual. Crime in the area was also up, with reports of chickens and other farm animals being stolen and sometimes found later in mutilated condition, along with wild animals such as raccoons and opossums. In a ditch along Willow Road, a dozen or so animal carcasses were found in a ditch. An 11-year-old child who lived in a house along Bowers Road (near

## WEREWOLVES AT THE MOVIES

One of the best ways to overcome an irrational fear of werewolves is familiarity. By exposing yourself to them repeatedly, you'll learn not to panic in their presence. Of course, exposing yourself to an actual werewolf, even if you can find one, has its drawbacks. A great alternative, especially since werewolves have been among of Hollywood's favorite B-movie staples for nearly a century, is werewolf movies, which range from serious film art to complete crap. Here are the DVDs to rent first:

*Werewolf of London* (1935)—The first werewolf movie ever made.

*The Wolf Man* (1941)—Lon Chaney Jr.'s classic werewolf portrayal is considered by fright-film buffs to be among the finest horror flicks ever made.

*I Was a Teenage Werewolf* (1957)—Michael Landon's portrayal of a teen transformed into a werewolf by his psychotherapist rose from the morass of '50s drive-in fodder to become a cult classic.

*An American Werewolf in London* (1981)—Director John Landis *(Animal House)* pays homage to the genre with this fine, very scary movie punctuated with weird comic relief.

Bray Road) saw a large dog that stood up and moved with great speed on two legs. Some claimed it was a coyote, though they readily admitted they had never seen one run on two legs.

*Wolfen* (1981)—This stylish allegory in the werewolf film revival of the early '80s features Albert Finney as a cop tracking a suspected werewolf through London. Great cinematography.

*Wolf* (1994)—Jack Nicholson delivers the greatest werewolf portrayal ever in this wry, satirical, darkly funny and grossly gory film by Mike Nichols about a mild-mannered New York editor who, bitten by a werewolf, turns proactive about office politics by eating his enemies. Excellent.

*Harry Potter and the Prisoner of Azkaban / Half-Blood Prince / Order of the Phoenix* (2004–2007)—J.K. Rowling gives us her take on werewolfery with one of her more intriguing characters, Defense Against the Dark Arts Professor Remus Lupin.

*Twilight / New Moon / Eclipse* (2008–2010)—Bella goes all mushy over Jake Black, an American Indian werewolf on a motorcycle. Huh? Find an adolescent girl to explain it all to you.

And if all else fails to assuage your fear of werewolves, watch *The Color of Money*, which has absolutely nothing to do with lycanthropy except for pool hustler Tom Cruise showing off to the music of the late rocker Warren Zevon's anthem "Werewolves of London": . . . "Better stay away from him. / He'll rip your lungs out, Jim. / (I'd like to meet his tailor.)"

Once the media got hold of the stories, tourists began to arrive with the locals selling monster T-shirts and "Beware of Werewolf" signs. Things eventually settled down and the visitors went back to where they'd come from, but the murders were still unsolved, and the locals were still apprehensive. A one point, John Frederickson stated that he believed several of the animals had been used in some sort of cult rituals. Police Chief James Larsen downplayed this idea, even though ropes had been tied around the back legs of some carcasses and their throats had been slit open. A few of the animals were decapitated and dismembered. The most recently slaughtered discovery was a dog that had had it's heart torn out. The crime scene was literally covered up when the area was bulldozed flat, concluding Frederickson's investigation.

A local dairy farmer, Scott Bray, reported seeing a strange-looking dog larger than a german shepherd in one of his pastures near Bray Road. It was covered in long gray-black hair and had a barrel chest. He followed it to a large pile of rocks, but it disappeared into the tall grass of the pasture on the other side. The Bray Road name stuck, and the rumors became legend.

Suddenly all sorts of crackpot theories began to emerge involving the collusion of satanic rituals and the Beast of Bray Road. Occult graffiti was found in an abandoned house and in the graveyard, where melted wax from candles had been dripped on the tombstones where the rituals had supposed taken place.

In 1991, Doris Gipson sighted the beast while driving near Delavan, Wisconsin, about 30 miles from the spot where Mark Shackelman originally sighted the beast in 1936. A large, hairy creature ran toward her vehicle and leaped onto her trunk. She would later compare the figure to a bodybuilder who worked out with weights. The markings in the paint do show that some sort of strange scratching activity took place. Was this the return of the werewolf?

Various comments from people over the years who have seen one of these beasts include:

"It was scary as hell."

"I never want to see this type of thing ever again."

"My desire for long, leisurely walks in the woods
    has been severly curtailed since the experience."

". . . Never went back to that place again."

"I have no idea what that thing was, I just know it wasn't a pleasant experience."

"I met tons (and I mean *tons*) of people in the area who also sighted similar things but are too embarrassed to admit it openly."

"I am really happy now to live in town."

But time has passed. The case has grown cold. Since 1992, there have been no credible reports of the beast, and at least until he makes another appearance, we may never know the truth.

# Timeline of the Werewolf

**75,000 BC**    Earliest human altars show evidence of prehistoric bear-worship cults

**10,000 BC**    Domestication of dogs

**6,000 BC**    Catal Huyuk cave drawings depict leopard-men hunting

**2,000 BC**    *Epic of Gilgamesh* contains first literary evidence of werewolves

**850 BC**    *The Odyssey* written down, including many traces of werewolf beliefs

| | |
|---|---|
| **500 BC** | Scythians record belief that the Neuri are werewolves |
| **400 BC** | Damarchus, an Arcadian werewolf, wins boxing medal at Olympic games |
| **100–75 BC** | Virgil's eighth ecologue describes voluntary transformation of werewolf |
| **AD 55** | Petronius writes about werewolves in Satyricon |
| **150** | Apuleius composes *The Metamorphoses* |
| **170** | Pausanias visits Arcadia and hears of Lykanian werewolf rites |
| **600** | Saint Albeus (Irish) said to have been suckled by wolves |
| **617** | Wolves said to have attacked heretical monks |
| **650** | Paulus Aegineta describes mental disorder of "melancholic lycanthropia" |
| **900** | Hrafnsmal mentions "wolf coats" among the Norwegian Army; Canon Episcopi |

condems the belief in reality of witches and werewolves as heretical

**1020**  First recorded use of the word *werewulf* in English

**1101**  Death of Ukrainian Prince Vseslav of Polotsk, alleged werewolf

**1182–1183**  Giraldus discovers Irish werewolf couple

**1194–1197**  Epic poem *Guillaume de Palerne* features friendly werewolf

**1198**  Marie de France's poem "Bisclavret" depicts werewolf with cheating wife

**1250**  Anonymous Lai de Melion tells of werewolf knight with unfaithful wife

**1275–1300**  *Volsungasaga*, Germanic werewolf saga, written

**1344**  Wolf-boy of Hesse discovered

**1347–1351**  First major outbreak of the Black Plague

**1407**  Werewolves mentioned during witchcraft trial at Basel

**1450**     Else of Meerburg accused of riding a wolf

**1486**     *Malleus Maleficarum* published, setting parameters for werewolf trials

**1494**     Swiss woman tried for riding a wolf

**1495**     Woman tried for riding a wolf at Lucerne

**1521**     Werewolves of Poligny burned

**1541**     Paduan werewolf dies after having arms and legs cut off

**1550**     Witekind interviews self-confessed werewolf at Riga

**1552**     Modern French version of *Guillaume* published at Lyon

**1555**     Olaus Magnus records strange behavior of Baltic werewolves

**1573**     Gilles Garnier burned as werewolf

**1575**     Trials of the Benandanti werewolves begin in Italy and continue for a century

**1584**       Reginald Scot's *Discoverie of Witchcraft* published

**1588**       Trial of first female werewolf in Auvergne

**1589**       Peter Stumpp executed as werewolf at Cologne

**1598**       Roulet tried as werewolf—sentence commuted; Werewolf of Chalons executed at Paris; Gandillon family burned as werewolves in the Jura

**1603**       Jean Grenier tried as werewolf, sentenced to life imprisonment

**1610**       Two women condemned as werewolves at Liege; Jean Grenier dies

**1637**       Famine in Franche-Comte; cannibalism reported

**1652**       Cromwellian law forbids export of Irish wolfhounds

**1692**       Livonian werewolf Theiss interrogated

| 1697 | Perrault's Contes includes "Little Red Riding Hood" |
| 1764 | Bete de Gevaudon starts werewolf scare in Auvergne |
| 1796–1799 | Widespread fear of wolves and werewolves reported in France |
| 1797 | Victor of Aveyron first seen |
| 1812 | Brothers Grimm publish their version of "Little Red Riding Hood" |
| 1824 | Antoine Leger tried for werewolf crimes and sentenced to lunatic asylum |
| 1886 | Robert Louis Stevenson's *Dr. Jekyll and Mr. Hyde* published |
| 1914 | Freud publishes paper about his "Wolf Man" patient |
| 1920 | Orissa's feral "wolf children" Kamala and Amala discovered; right-wing terror group "Operation Werewolf" established in Germany |

| | |
|---|---|
| **1936** | First sighting of the Wisconsin werewolf by Mark Shackelman |
| **1951** | Outbreak of hallucinogenic ergotism at Pont-Saint-Esprit |
| **1952** | Ogburn & Bose's *On the Trail of the Wolf-Children* published |
| **1970** | Four teenagers spot werewolf alongside road in Gallup, New Mexico |
| **1971** | Female werewolf seen in Mobile, Alabama |
| **1972** | Feral child Shamdeo discovered living among wolves in India |
| **1975** | Surawicz and Banta publish first two modern cases of lycanthopy; Celtic stone heads found in Hexham, England summon a werewolf |
| **1980** | High school kids sight werewolf in Manitoba, Canada |
| **1986** | Large were-beast seen in Manistee, Michigan |

| | |
|---|---|
| **1988** | Monsieur X arrested; McLean Hospital survey published; werewolf returns to Wittlich, Germany |
| **1989** | First sighting of the Beast of Bray Road |
| **1992** | Most recent sighting of Wisconsin's Beast of Bray Road |
| **1994** | Skinwalker Ranch in Utah becomes the site of extreme paranormal activity |
| **1997** | Werewolf seen outside of Asheville, North Carolina |
| **1998** | Young man at campsite in Albuquerque, New Mexico, sights skinwalker |
| **2000** | Pack of werewolves heard forging a stream in Kentucky |
| **2006** | Dog Man of Michigan sighted multiple times |
| **2010** | Pennsylvania teacher Candice Berner attacked and killed in "rare" wolf attack |

# Bibliography

Ashley, Leonard R. N.: *The Complete Book of Werewolves* (Barricade Books, 2001)

Asma, Stephen T.: *On Monsters* (Oxford University Press, 2009)

Barber, Paul: *Vampires, Burial, and Death* (Yale University Press, 1988)

Baring-Gould, Sabine: *The Book of Were-Wolves* (Causeway Books, 1973)

Borges, Jorge Luis: *The Book of Imaginary Beings* (Avon, 1969)

Brooks, Max: *The Zombie Survival Guide* (Three Rivers Press, 2003)

Brown, Nathan Robert: *The Complete Idiot's Guide to Werewolves* (Alpha Books, 2009)

Copper, Basil: *The Werewolf in Legend, Fact and Art* (St. Martin's Press, 1977)

Curran, Dr. Bob: *Werewolves* (New Page Books, 2009)

Duncan, Ritch & Bob Powers: *The Werewolf's Guide to Life* (Broadway Books, 2009)

Glut, Donald F.: *True Werewolves of History* (Sense of Wonder Press, 2004)

Godfrey, Linda S.: *Hunting the American Werewolf* (Trails Media Group, 2006)

Greer, John Michael: *Monsters* (Llewellyn Publications, 2004)

Hogg, Garry: *Cannibalism and Human Sacrifice* (Robert Hale LTD, 1958)

Izzard, Jon: *Werewolves* (Spruce, 2009)

Masters, Anthony: *The Natural History of the Vampire* (G. P. Putnam's Sons, 1972)

Otten, Charlotte F. (ed.): *A Lycanthropy Reader: Werewolves in Western Culture* (Syracuse University Press, 1986)

Rudorff, Raymond: *Monsters* (Neville Spearman, 1968)

Senn, Harry A.: *Were-Wolf and Vampire in Romania* (Columbia University Press, 1982)

Steiger, Brad: *The Werewolf Book: The Encyclopedia of Shapeshifting Beings* (Visible Ink Press, 1999)

Summers, Montague: *The Werewolf* (University Books, 1966)

Plus the many blogs, e-mails and personal tales encountered on the World Wide Web

# Other Ulysses Press Books

### Bella Should Have Dumped Edward: Controversial Views & Debates on the Twilight Series
*Michelle Pan, $14.95*

Twilight expert Michelle Pan has teamed up with Twihards worldwide to create a book filled with fan perspectives on the hottest topics surrounding the vampire saga.

### Curse of the Full Moon: A Werewolf Anthology
*James Lowder, Editor, $14.95*

The stories in this book explore all elements of these intriguing creatures, from violent nocturnal transformations to torturous efforts to survive on the fringes of society.

### The Dead That Walk: Flesh-Eating Stories
*Stephen Jones, Editor, $14.95*

More than just brain-eating assaults, the tales in this anthology explore all elements of zombie existence and their interaction with the humans they live among.

### Vampires Don't Sleep Alone: Your Guide to Meeting, Dating and Seducing a Vampire
*Elizabeth Barrial & D. H. Altair, $12.95*

A deadly serious guide for anyone looking to seduce the most dangerous—and exciting—of sexual playmates.

### Visitants: Stories of Fallen Angels and Heavenly Hosts

*Stephen Jones, Editor, $14.95*

This collection of stories about the new angels—youthful, immortal and powerful—includes romantic entanglements with winged bad boys, devilish interventions with evil messengers, and bloody battles against ravaging demons.

### The Zombie Handbook: How to Identify the Living Dead & Survive the Coming Zombie Apocalypse

*Rob Sacchetto, $16.95*

This book reveals the vital information that (human) readers need to know about identifying, understanding and, when things get ugly, dispatching the "living dead."

### Zombiewood Weekly: The Celebrity Dead Exposed

*Rob Sacchetto, $14.95*

In this paparazzi-inspired collection of images, America's bad and beautiful are revealed as never before—in their undisguised, flesh-rotting, zombified, day-to-day existence.

*To order these books call 800-377-2542 or 510-601-8301, fax 510-601-8307, e-mail ulysses@ulyssespress.com, or write to Ulysses Press, P.O. Box 3440, Berkeley, CA 94703. All retail orders are shipped free of charge. California residents must include sales tax. Allow two to three weeks for delivery.*

# About the Author

**DEL HOWISON** is a three-time nominated Bram Stoker Award–winning editor and author. He has been nominated for a Shirley Jackson Award, a Rondo Hatton Award and the Black Quill Award. His short stories have appeared in various anthologies throughout the years, and his tale "The Lost Herd" was converted into a script by Mick Garris and filmed as the premiere episode of the NBC horror anthology series *Fear Itself*.